How to Find Lost Treasure in All Fifty States
and Canada, too!

by Joan Holub

ALADDIN PAPERBACKS
New York   London   Toronto   Sydney   Singapore

First Aladdin Paperbacks edition June 2000

Aladdin Paperbacks
An imprint of Simon & Schuster Children's Publishing Division
1230 Avenue of the Americas
New York, NY 10020

The text for this book was set in Stone Informal.
Book design by Corinne Allen
Printed and bound in the United States of America
10 9 8 7 6 5 4 3 2 1

Library of Congress Cataloging-in-Publication Data
Holub, Joan.
How to find lost treasure in all fifty states and Canada, too! / Joan Holub.
—1st Aladdin Paperbacks ed.
p.   cm.
Summary: Describes treasures that have been lost in each of the fifty states and in various locations in Canada.
ISBN 0-689-82643-5 (pbk.)
1. United States—History, Local Anecdotes—Juvenile literature.
2. Canada—History, Local Anecdotes—Juvenile literature.
3. Treasure-trove—United States—History, Anecdotes—Juvenile literature.
4. Treasure-trove—Canada—History, Anecdotes—Juvenile literature.
[1. Buried treasure. 2. United States—History. 3. Canada—History.]
I. Title.
E179.H825   2000
973-dc21   99-27669
CIP

For George Hallowell, who visited Oak Island, and gave me the idea for this book. —J. H.

Author's Note: With each retelling of a lost treasure story, the facts may change until no one is sure exactly how or where a treasure was lost. More than one version of a lost treasure tale may evolve over time. In this book, I have tried to retell the version that is most often repeated or that seems most logical. Treasure hunters should further research the facts of each legend and all laws governing treasure hunting for themselves before searching for any lost treasures.

Contents

Introduction

Is there a lost treasure where you live?

Yes! There are lost treasures in every state in the United States and all over the world. Treasures can be hidden underground, in swamps, oceans, caves, houses, and even backyards. Lost treasures could be just about anywhere!

How does treasure get lost?

Nobody loses a treasure on purpose. So how do so many get lost?

Before there were banks, some people kept their money and jewels safe by burying them. Miners often hid their gold and silver underground or in caves while they dug for more. They all wanted their hiding places to be secret. Sometimes they didn't tell anyone where it was—not even their families. When they died, no one knew where their treasures were hidden.

Pirates who robbed ships could not put their stolen booty in a bank. Neither could outlaws who robbed banks, trains, or stagecoaches. They sometimes hid it. Often they died or went to jail before they could go back for their treasure.

Have you ever hidden something and then forgotten where it was? Imagine if you buried a treasure but couldn't find it when you went back to look. This has really happened!

The stories surrounding lost treasures are mysterious. Not everyone agrees on the facts of how some treasures were lost, who they belong to, what the treasures are worth, or even if all stories of lost treasure are true. Many treasure hunters believe the treasures in this book are real. But they don't know exactly where or how to find them. Will you be the one to figure out where a treasure is hidden?

Alabama
The Inca Gold of Red Bone Cave

The treasure: Millions of dollars' worth of Inca and/or American Indian gold and jewelry

Where it is: In a limestone cave north of the Tennessee River, near Muscle Shoals, Alabama

In 1532, a Spanish explorer named Hernando de Soto sailed across the Atlantic Ocean to South America searching for gold and silver. He and his men found a wealth of Inca gold in Peru. Many researchers believe that he took this gold back to Spain in 1536, and then returned to North America years later. But according to a well-known treasure legend, de Soto took Peru's Inca gold with him directly from South America to North America instead.

Most researchers do agree that de Soto first landed in Florida in May 1539, probably near Tampa Bay. He soon began exploring the southeastern United States, and is credited with discovering the Mississippi River. Some treasure hunters think that de Soto found more gold during this time. Others don't think he had any luck finding gold in North America.

In 1540, de Soto and his men decided to camp for the winter in northeastern Alabama, along the Tennessee River. The nearby Chickasaw Indians were friendly and gave them gifts. In return, de Soto gave them pork to eat. A few Chickasaw liked it so much that they tried to take more of the Spaniards' pigs. De Soto's men caught and punished the thieves. Then they told the Chickasaw chief to give them some servants. All of this made the chief so angry that he and his tribe attacked and killed many of the Spaniards. De Soto escaped, but died on May 21, 1542, and was buried in the waters of the Mississippi River.

The Spaniards' gold was left behind. The Chickasaw didn't use gold for money. But they knew that gold was important to the explorers who were invading their land. Others would come if they heard about the gold, and the Indians didn't want that to happen. They hid the gold in one of the many caves along the Tennessee River, and kept it a secret.

Over time, there were rumors about the lost gold among settlers, trappers, and hunters in the area. But no one knew if the gold was real or where to find it. The Chickasaw used small amounts of the gold to make jewelry, but the gold itself remained safely hidden for many years.

In the early 1700s, a trapper visited the Chickasaw village and was allowed to live there while he trapped and hunted. The chief's daughter quickly fell in love with him. After he had been in the Indian village for a few weeks, the trapper was kidnapped from his bed one night. He was blindfolded, led through the forest,

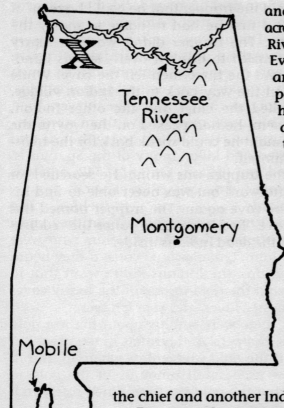

and then taken across the Tennessee River in a canoe. Eventually, he and his kidnappers climbed a hill and entered a cave. The trapper was taken deep inside the cave, walking for ten minutes or so. Suddenly, his blindfold was removed. He was surprised to find that his kidnappers were the chief and another Indian.

Even more amazing—the trapper saw gold all around him! There were gold and silver bars stacked to the ceiling, as well as old wooden chests full of gold coins and jewels. There were also Indian skeletons. The Chickasaw believed that the spirits of these dead men were guarding the treasure.

The chief told the trapper that he could have all of the treasure. But first he had to agree to marry the chief's daughter. The trapper didn't want to marry her, but he promised to think it over. He was blindfolded again, and the three men left the cave. While they camped on the way back to the Indian village, the trapper killed the chief and the other Indian. Unknown to them, he had peeked on the way to the cave. So he thought he could sneak back for the treasure again by himself.

However, the trapper was wrong. He searched for many years afterward but was never able to find his way back to the cave again. The trapper named this lost treasure cave "Red Bone Cave" after the reddish-colored skin of the dead Indians inside.

Alaska
The Lake of the Golden Bar Treasure

The treasure: About five hundred pounds of gold nuggets

Where it is: The Saint Elias Mountains

Around 1883, prospectors got lucky as they searched for gold in the Saint Elias Mountains of Alaska. Along the edge of a small lake they found huge gold nuggets. Some weighed as much as fifty pounds! The prospectors mined the area for many months, gathering over five hundred pounds of gold. They built a small cabin to live in and hid their gold in a small, nearby cave.

According to legend, they were killed in a terrific blizzard and eventually eaten by grizzly bears. They never got a chance to take their gold into town and spend any of it.

Among their remains, a diary was found. It had been written by one of the prospectors. The diary mentioned the treasure but did not reveal the exact location. This is the only lead to this treasure.

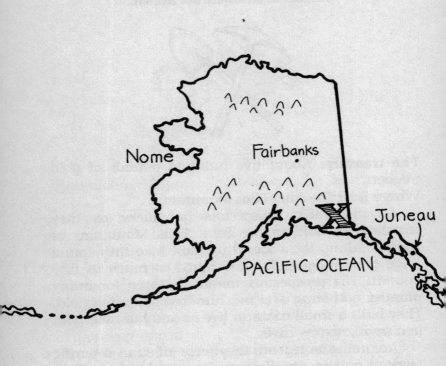

Arizona
The Legend of the Lost Dutchman Mine

The treasure: Gold mine

Where it is: The Superstition Mountains, about thirty-five miles east of Phoenix, Arizona

The Lost Dutchman Mine is one of the most famous treasure legends in the United States. This lost gold mine is nicknamed after Jacob Waltz, though he was actually German rather than Dutch.

Waltz came to the United States somewhere between 1839 and 1862 and began mining near Phoenix, Arizona, in 1867. He probably discovered his gold mine in the 1870s. When he began spending lots of money around town, rumors of his gold strike quickly spread. But Waltz was careful never to let anyone follow him to his mine, so no one learned its whereabouts.

In Jacob Waltz's time, there was a tradition of telling your secrets before you died. So as he lay dying at the home of Julia Thomas in 1891, Waltz told a treasure tale to those at his bedside. He told them that he had indeed discovered a rich gold mine in the

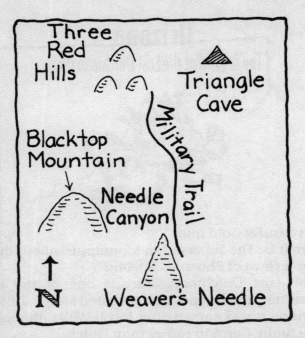

Three
Red
Hills

Triangle
Cave

Military Trail

Blacktop
Mountain

Needle
Canyon

N

Weavers Needle

Superstition Mountains. To prove it, he pulled a box from under his bed. There were nearly fifty pounds of gold inside!

Did Waltz actually mine the gold, or had he discovered gold mined and left behind by earlier Spanish, Mexican, or American miners? All three had explored the area in the past, but many treasure hunters believe that the gold was originally mined by Mexicans.

In the 1840s, a treaty had been signed making the Superstition Mountains part of the United States instead of Mexico. A wealthy Mexican family named Peralta was mining gold in these mountains at that time. They planned to move it all to Mexico before

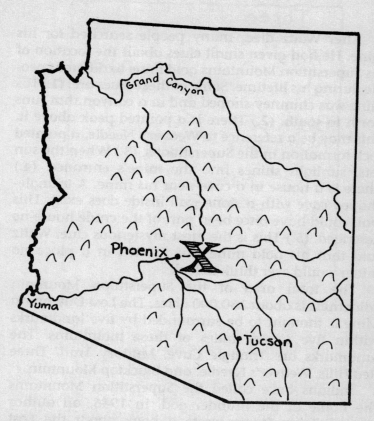

the treaty took effect. However, Apaches attacked and killed them before they could. The Indians had no use for the gold, so they left it behind. Was this the gold Waltz had found? Only one of the nuggets he gave the men when he died is still around today. Some gold experts say that Waltz's gold has no known source, so it is likely that it's from a mine that remains undiscovered.

After Waltz died, many people searched for his mine. He had given small clues about the location of his Superstition Mountains gold mine to different people during his lifetime. Some of these clues are: (1.) His mine was chimney-shaped and in a canyon that runs north to south. (2.) There is a pointed peak above it. This may be a reference to Weaver's Needle, a pointed rock formation in the Superstitions. (3.) When the sun sets, sunlight shines into the mine's entrance. (4.) There is a house in a cave near his mine. A triangle-shaped cave with a stone wall inside does exist. This wall could have once been part of the crude house he described. (5.) This is the most mysterious clue: Waltz said that his gold mine was located in a place no miner would ever think to look.

The total area of the Superstition Mountain wilderness is about 160,000 acres. The Lost Dutchman Mine is thought to be surrounded by five landmarks within five square miles of these mountains. The landmarks are Triangle Cave, Military Trail, Three Red Hills, Weaver's Needle, and Blacktop Mountain.

Indians once called the Superstition Mountains the home of the thunder god. In 1946, an author named Barry Storm wrote a book about the Lost Dutchman Mine called *Thunder Gods' Gold!* In 1949 it was made into a Hollywood movie called *Lust for Gold.* Facts in the book and movie were not completely accurate, but they interested many people in the search for this mine.

Miners have spent decades searching for this treasure, and as many as one hundred lives have been lost in the search. Some treasure hunters think that an 1887 earthquake may have buried the mine, but no one is certain. Mining is not allowed in the Superstition Mountains today, but some still search for this great treasure.

Arkansas
Silver Bullet Treasure

The treasure: Silver mine
Where it is: Moccasin Creek Valley, near Dover, Arkansas

In 1903, a poor farmer named Tobe Inmon took his son to a doctor. The doctor cured his son's fever, but Inmon had no money to pay his fee. He offered to pay the doctor with a bag of bullets instead. Bullets were valuable and hard to find in those days, so the doctor gladly accepted. Inmon told the doctor that he had made the bullets out of lead he found in an old mine in the hills near his cabin. He and his family lived in a one-room log cabin in Moccasin Creek Valley outside Dover, Arkansas.

Two years later, the doctor opened the bag of bullets to use on a deer hunt. When he scratched some of the bullets, he realized they were made of silver rather than lead. The doctor rode to Inmon's farm to tell him the exciting news. He imagined they would both soon be rich. But to his surprise, Inmon's farm was deserted. None of his neighbors knew where he and his family

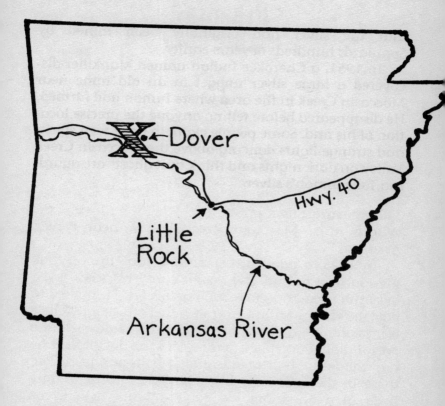

Dover

Hwy. 40

Little
Rock

Arkansas River

had moved, but some thought they'd gone to Texas. The doctor gave up his medical practice and spent the rest of his life searching for the silver mine. He went broke and died without ever finding it.

In spite of the fact that the doctor was unsuccessful, many other treasure hunters have since taken up the hunt for Inmon's silver. Spanish mining tools have been found in the area of his farm. This could mean that the silver had originally been mined by Spaniards hundreds of years earlier.

In 1951, a Cherokee Indian named Mankiller discovered a large silver nugget in an old mine near Moccasin Creek in the area where Inmon had farmed. He disappeared before telling anyone the precise location of his find. Some people claim to have seen spirits and strange lights dancing above the Moccasin Creek Valley on dark nights and think that ghosts are guarding Tobe Inmon's silver.

California
Lost Death Valley Gold

The treasure: Millions of dollars' worth of gold ore
Where it is: The Funeral Mountain Range, in Death Valley, California

The discovery of gold in California began the gold rush in the United States. In January of 1848, James Marshall found gold in a mill pond while building a sawmill for a man named John Sutter. Word leaked out, and a year later (in 1849), thousands of miners rushed westward to California.

Around 1862, a California businessman named Charles Breyfogle heard that gold and silver had been discovered near Austin, Nevada. Hoping to strike it rich, he and two other prospectors left Los Angeles on foot and headed across the Mojave Desert, toward Nevada. They were in a hurry, so they chose the shortest route. It was also the most dangerous one. One night, they camped on the east side of the Panamint Mountains. The next day they would reach Death Valley. Breyfogle camped a distance away from the others, where he found a more comfortable sleeping

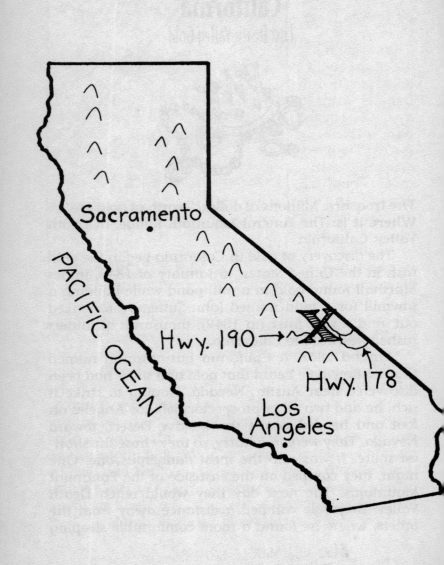

PACIFIC OCEAN

Sacramento

Hwy. 190 →

Hwy. 178

Los Angeles

place with fewer rocks.

In the middle of the night, Breyfogle heard Indians attack and kill his two partners. Breyfogle grabbed his shoes, but he was so terrified that he did not even take time to put them on. He escaped before the Indians noticed next morning,

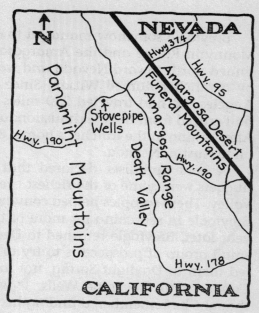

his feet so badly cut and swollen that his shoes would not fit. He didn't know what direction he had run and was soon lost. Barefoot and in pain, he wandered out of the Panamint Mountains, through Death Valley, and into the Funeral Mountains.

While searching for water, Breyfogle stumbled across a shiny rock. It was gold! The source was a two-foot-thick gold vein about twenty yards away. He filled his bandanna with as many of the gold nuggets as he could carry. By this time, he was tired and lost. Still, he tried to take note of his surroundings so he could return for more gold someday. He noticed a small mesquite tree nearby, and a water hole, where he drank.

Breyfogle somehow managed to cross the Funeral Mountain Range and the Amargosa Desert. He continued north toward Nevada and was finally rescued by a rancher named Wilson. Since first leaving Los Angeles, he had traveled 250 miles on foot! He was half-crazed from heat, exhaustion, and lack of water. After resting at the rancher's home, Breyfogle traveled on to Austin, Nevada.

A gold appraiser declared that Breyfogle's gold nuggets were some of the richest ever found in Death Valley. These samples helped convince others to assist Breyfogle in searching for more of the gold. About a year later, Breyfogle returned to Death Valley with a small group of prospectors to try to find it again. He led them to Daylight Spring, not far from Boundary Canyon and Stovepipe Wells. It was there that he thought he remembered finding his gold. But he had been delirious at the time. It was difficult for him to remember everything clearly. He was able to find the bones of his two friends, who had been killed by the Indians. He also found the water hole where he had drunk, and the small mesquite he remembered. But he could not find the gold. Little did he know that a few months after his rescue, heavy rains in the area had caused a landslide that may have buried his gold.

The rest of the group eventually gave up and returned to Nevada, but Breyfogle continued searching alone. Though he hunted until his death in 1870, he never found his gold again.

Many others have looked for Breyfogle's gold, too. Even George Hearst, father of the well-known publisher, William Randolph Hearst, once helped finance a search. The exact location of Breyfogle's famous gold discovery remains a mystery. Many have tried, but no one has been able to find it.

Colorado
Missing Treasure Mountain Gold

The treasure: An estimated $50 million' worth of gold ore
Where it is: The San Juan Mountains of southern Colorado, near Wolf Creek Pass, west of Summitville

In 1800, a group of French prospectors found a Spanish treasure map. The map led them to strike gold in the San Juan Mountains of Colorado. After mining for several years, the Frenchmen had a huge stockpile of gold. They were ready to take it to the port at New Orleans, Louisiana, where it could then be shipped on to France.

Spanish miners in the area heard about the French gold and plotted to steal it. The Spanish promised local Indians that they would pay for French scalps. Indian attacks soon became a constant threat to the French miners. The Spanish plan to drive the French away was working.

The French miners decided to hide their treasure in one of the mine shafts. They hoped to return for it later, once the Indian threat had ended. The mine shaft they chose as a hiding place went straight down

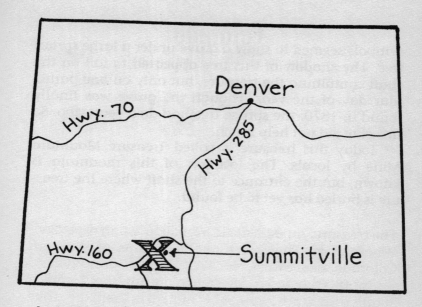

about thirty feet and then turned horizontal for about fifty more feet. The French stored their gold deep in the horizontal part of the tunnel and filled the vertical part with rocks to disguise it.

But they didn't get out in time. All of the French miners except a man named Remy LeDoux (or Labreau) were killed during yet another Indian attack. LeDoux returned to France alone with a map showing the location of the treasure.

Other treasure hunters used LeDoux's map to search for the gold around 1844. They found the French mine but they could not find the exact shaft where the gold had been hidden. The prospectors had nearly given up the search when one of them noticed symbols on the map that might be clues. These symbols seemed to show a grave under a large spruce tree. The shadow of this tree appeared to fall on the shaft containing the treasure, but only on one particular day of the year. Though the grave was finally found in 1870, the spruce tree had died years ago. So this clue did not help much.

Today this treasure is called Treasure Mountain Mine by locals. The location of this mountain is known, but the entrance to the shaft where the treasure is buried has yet to be found.

Connecticut
The Buried Treasure of Pirate Captain Kidd

The treasure: An unknown amount of fabulous pirate loot

Where it is: Old Lyme, Money Island, Stratford Point, and Clarke's Island

Captain William Kidd was hired as a privateer by King William III of England in 1695. Privateers were sea captains sailing privately owned ships who were hired by a country's government to attack its enemies. Kidd's first mission as a privateer for England was to capture pirates. He sailed westward from England in a ship called the *Adventure Galley.* His first stop in America was New York, where he hired more crewmen. He was forced to hire unsavory men, since he couldn't find many good men willing to go on a long voyage.

Months passed before he finally left New York and began his mission. By then, the pirates he was chasing had heard that he was coming, and fled. Kidd followed them around the Cape of Good Hope at the southern tip of Africa and northward into the Indian

Ocean. His food and supplies were soon running low, and he had yet to capture any pirates. Kidd's crew was hungry and tired of working for little or no pay. They mutinied and forced him to become a pirate himself.

After three years of pirating in the Indian Ocean, Kidd returned to his home and family in New York. He asked the English king to pardon him. Instead, Kidd was put on trial for piracy. He was found guilty and hanged in London, England, on May 23, 1701. His body was covered with tar and hung in public as a warning to other pirates.

Even though Captain Kidd is one of the most famous pirates of all time, some people believe he wasn't a pirate at all. They think he was only trying to follow the king's orders in everything he did on the seas.

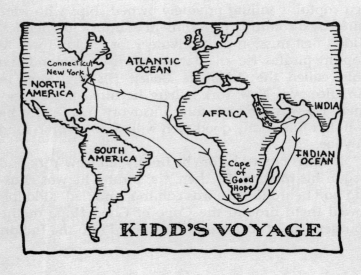

KIDD'S VOYAGE

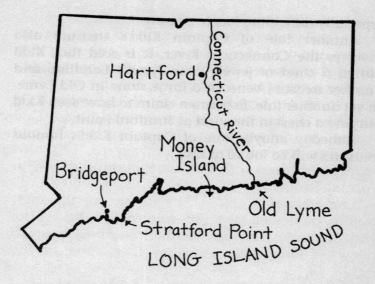

Hartford

Connecticut River

Money Island

Bridgeport

Old Lyme

Stratford Point

LONG ISLAND SOUND

There are many stories that Captain Kidd buried treasure along the East Coast of the United States. No treasure has ever been found, and no one knows if these stories are true. But there are more buried treasure stories about Captain Kidd than about any other pirate.

One such tale is that Kidd and another pirate named Clarke buried two chests filled with gold, jewels, and other wealth worth about half a million dollars on Clarke's Island in the Connecticut River. After Kidd's hanging, his lawyer searched for this treasure. Although the lawyer found clues, he failed to find the treasure itself. Since Captain Kidd's death, the Connecticut River has changed course and new trees have grown up. As a result, this treasure may be especially difficult to locate by now.

Another tale of Captain Kidd's treasure also involves the Connecticut River. It is said that Kidd buried a chest of jewels near Tyron's Landing, and another treasure beneath a large stone in Old Lyme. In yet another tale, fishermen claim to have seen Kidd burying a chest in the sand at Stratford Point.

Someday, maybe one of Captain Kidd's famous treasures will be found at last!

Delaware
Revolutionary War Gold Coins

The treasure: An iron pot full of gold coins
Where it is: Purgatory Woods, near Cooch's Bridge, along the Christina River

The only Revolutionary War battle ever fought in Delaware was known as the Battle of Cooch's Bridge. In August 1777, British troops were advancing north toward Philadelphia. General George Washington ordered American troops to delay the British army so that he would have more time to organize defenses north of them. American General William Maxwell was following these orders on September 3, 1777, when he met British forces on Cooch's Bridge over the Christina River in Delaware.

A man named Thomas Cooch owned a mill and house located at this bridge. He worriedly watched the American and British troops gather. The closer the troops got to his mill, the more concerned he grew. Would his home soon become the scene of a battle? Just in case, Cooch decided to hide his family's valuables for safekeeping. He packed their silver and jewels

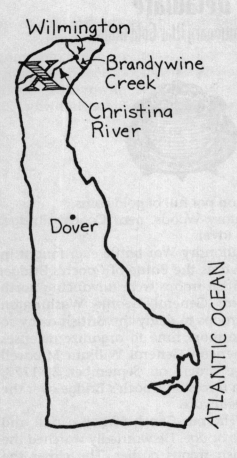

Wilmington

Brandywine Creek

Christina River

Dover

ATLANTIC OCEAN

into a chest, and filled an iron pot with gold coins. Just as the American and British troops began to battle on the bridge, Cooch took his treasure into the nearby Purgatory Woods. He buried the chest and pot separately there in a marshy area.

The troops battled on, but the Americans were eventually forced to retreat. When all the cannon and musket fire had finally died down, Cooch was shocked by what he saw. A fire had destroyed his mill and the part of Purgatory Woods where his treasure was hidden. He hurried to look for his buried fortune, and was able to find his chest of silver and jewels. But the markings he had made to show the location of his iron pot of coins had been lost in the fire. Try as he might, he was unable to find the coin-filled pot.

Thomas Cooch's iron pot full of gold coins may still be hidden somewhere near Cooch's Bridge today. The bridge is located on State Highway 281, about half a mile from where it intersects State Highway 72.

Florida
Shipwrecked Treasures

The treasure: Millions of dollars' worth of sunken treasure

Where it is: On sunken ships along the coast of Florida

Some amazing lost treasures lie waiting to be found on as many as two thousand shipwrecks along the coast of Florida. Why did so many ships sink in this area? From the 1500s through the early 1800s, Spain sent many ships to the New World (America) to search for gold and silver. Spanish ships, called galleons, were top-heavy and overturned easily in the hurricanes and storms that are common in Florida waters.

Sailors kept a careful eye on the weather and tried to avoid storms. They believed that when their bones ached, a storm was coming. If the ocean was very calm for days and the water was clear, they thought this was a sign that a hurricane was on the way. But this system of weather prediction was far from perfect, and weather was a constant danger along the Florida coast.

Just south of Florida are small islands called the Florida Keys. When sailing along the Keys and the Florida coast, ships tried to stay close enough to shore to see the coastline. This was necessary so they'd know where they were. Because the world had not been fully explored yet, maps and charts were often wrong. A compass helped, but keeping in sight of land was the best way to stay on course. Still, it was dangerous to sail so close to the coastline because ships could easily run into rocks in shallow water. Many ships sank along the Florida coast in this way.

The return trip back from the New World to Spain was especially dangerous. Ships were often in bad condition after a long voyage, and their sides were covered with barnacles and moss. As the Dutch, English, and French also began to travel to the New World, still more ships sank.

It is hard to know exactly what treasures might exist on sunken ships. Although each ship's captain kept a

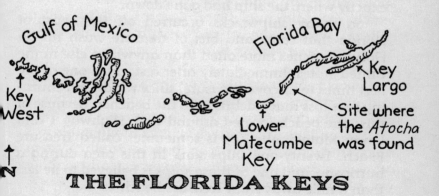

THE FLORIDA KEYS

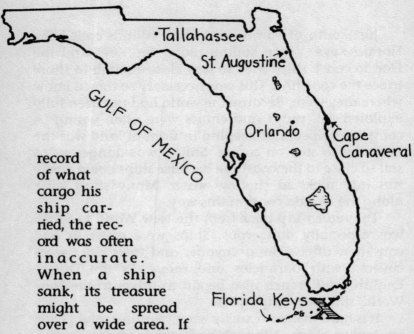

record of what cargo his ship carried, the record was often inaccurate. When a ship sank, its treasure might be spread over a wide area. If everyone aboard a ship died, there was no one to tell exactly where the ship had gone down.

So many shipwrecks occurred off the coast of Florida that coins and bits of treasure wash up on Florida beaches more often than anywhere else in the United States. Immediately after a storm is one of the best times to discover treasure, since winds and churning seas toss much debris onto the beaches. Because of this, one beach located around U. S. Highway 1 and Lower Matacumbe Key is sometimes called Treasure Beach. Twenty-one ships sank in this area during a hurricane, and one of those ships is believed to lie less than a mile away from Treasure Beach.

In 1985, a man named Mel Fisher salvaged a sunken Spanish galleon called the *Atocha*. The ship had sunk in a 1622 storm off the southern Florida coast. Its treasure cargo's value was estimated at $375 to $450 million, and is the greatest ever discovered on a Spanish ship.

Some other treasure ships that have sunk near Florida include:

The Spanish galleon *Santa Rosa,* which sank south of Key West in 1520. The ship was believed to carry $30 million' worth of Aztec gold as well as jewels. Treasure hunters tried to salvage this wreck in 1946, but failed.

The 250-ton Spanish galleon *La Madalena,* which sank during a storm in 1563 on the return voyage from the New World to Spain. The ship was said to carry 50 tons of silver and over 1100 pounds of gold, as well as jewelry.

Two rich Spanish galleons, the 300-ton *San Ignacio* and the *Santa Maria de la Limpia Concepción,* which were lost during a storm in 1571. Together, the ships carried over 2,500,000 pesos' worth of gold and silver. These shipwrecks took place somewhere near Saint Augustine or Cape Canaveral.

A 700-ton Spanish galleon, the *Santissima Concepción,* which went aground and was lost in shallow waters during a 1683 hurricane. It carried nearly 2,000,000 pesos' worth of gold, silver, pearls, emeralds, and other treasure.

Georgia
The Farmer's Round Treasure Map

The treasure: $100,000' worth of gold and silver coins
Where it is: About eight miles north of La Grange, Georgia

A wealthy Georgia farmer named Lipscombe had a problem: He had a lot of money but did not trust banks. In order to keep his money safe, he decided to bury it one night. Somewhere on the land near his house, Lipscombe and one of his slaves buried two treasures. They hid about $75,000' worth of gold coins in one place, and $25,000' worth of silver coins in another. Not even Lipscombe's family was allowed to know the secret locations.

As the Civil War began, Lipscombe became depressed, and his health grew worse. Worried that he might forget where his treasures were, he decided to make an unusual map on a decorative plate. He hammered a gold coin in the middle of one side of the heavy lead plate and carved an arrow pointing in the direction of the gold coins. Then he hammered a silver coin in the middle of the other side with an arrow

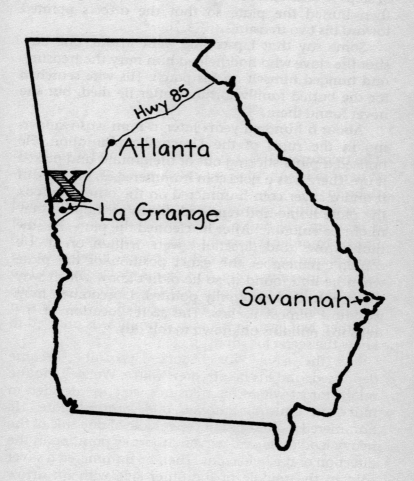

pointing to the silver coins. He also wrote the number of steps to take to reach each treasure on the plate. He then buried the plate so that the arrows pointed toward his two treasures.

Some say that Lipscombe went insane one day, shot the slave who had helped him bury the treasure, and hanged himself on his porch. His wife searched for the buried family fortunes after he died, but she never found them.

About a hundred years later, a man was wandering in the ruins of the Lipscombe plantation. He noticed a plate sticking out of the ground and picked it up. There was a gold coin hammered on one side of it and a silver coin hammered on the other. He took the plate home and removed the coins, hoping they might be valuable. After he cleaned the plate, he saw that arrows and directions were written on it. He couldn't remember the exact position of the plate when he had found it, so he didn't know which way the arrows had originally pointed. Lipscombe's map was now almost useless. The secret location of the treasures remains unknown to this day.

Hawaii
The Lost Treasure of King Kamehameha

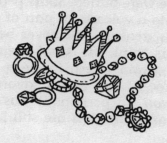

The treasure: Historic Hawaiian objects, King Kamehameha's robe, and gold
Where it is: Hawaiian Islands

The treasure of King Kamehameha (Kah-MAY-ha-MAY-ha) lies buried with his bones. King Kamehameha conquered the main island of Hawaii in 1782. By 1795, he had unified most of the Hawaiian Islands, which he ruled from 1795 to 1819. It was a peaceful and prosperous time for the islands. Kamehameha increased trade with other countries, and continued to follow the ancient religion and customs of Hawaii.

When he died on May 8, 1819, his chiefs buried him in the traditional way: They wrapped his bones with leaves and put them in a basket. Only chiefs were allowed to know where he was buried. No one else in the village was allowed to go outside while they took the basket to a secret burial spot. Along with the king's bones, the chiefs hid his beautiful feathered robes made from birds that are now extinct, part of his great treasure, and ancient Hawaiian objects.

No one today knows where King Kamehameha and his treasure were buried. Some people think they were thrown into a volcano as part of a ceremony. If that is true, his treasure will never be found. Other treasure hunters think the king's treasure is buried somewhere in a rain forest, inside a secret cave or underground room. The king's favorite island was mainland Hawaii, so perhaps it was chosen as his burial site. Treasure hunters are still looking for this treasure.

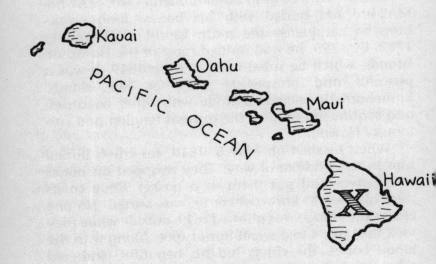

Idaho
Lost Treasure of the Lava Caves

The treasure: Two gold bars worth about $100,000
Where it is: Inside of a lava cave near Big Southern Butte

Around 1885, the owners of the Custer Mine near Big Lost River grew tired of having their gold stolen by stagecoach bandits. At one time the mine had been able to ship profits on the stagecoach safely. But recently there had been a rash of holdups. The mine owners decided to cast their gold in larger, heavier bars. They hoped this would make it more difficult for robbers on horseback to steal the gold.

Soon after they began making larger bars, one of their stagecoaches was traveling along a trail through Idaho's lava beds. It was carrying several passengers as well as two of the new large-size 125-pound gold bars from the Custer Mine. The stagecoach driver was forced to stop suddenly when he noticed some rocks blocking the trail ahead. It was a trap! A masked bandit darted out from behind a rock and pointed a gun at the driver. The bandit stole the gold and the passengers' jewelry.

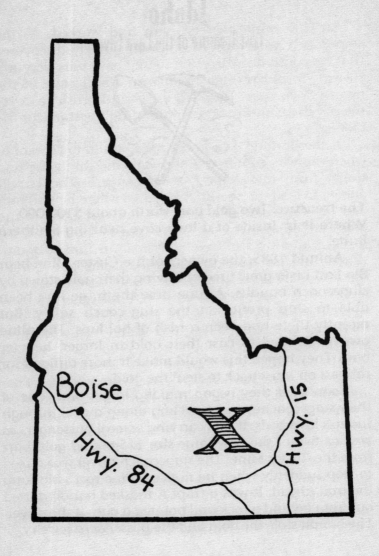

Boise

Hwy. 84

Hwy. 15

X

But the mine owners' plan had worked. As the stagecoach moved on, the bandit quickly discovered that he could not carry the heavy gold bars very far. He was forced to hide them in a small cave in the nearby lava rock. He piled rocks and brush to cover the cave's opening and left, planning to return for the loot later.

A sheriff and posse tracked the bandit to Montana, where he was captured along with the things he had stolen from the stagecoach passengers. The bandit agreed to lead the sheriff to the cave where he had hidden the Custer Mine's gold. On the way back to the gold, the bandit told the posse that he had left three markers around the cave to help him find it again. When they arrived at the holdup site, the bandit quickly pointed out the first marker. But then he pretended to be confused about where his other markers were. The posse divided up to search. The wily bandit managed to escape during the search and was never seen again.

Around 1915, a man from New Mexico arrived in Idaho with a treasure map. It showed the location of the lava cave that held the gold bars. He said it had been given to him by the stagecoach robber, who was afraid he'd be arrested if he returned to Idaho. However, there were many lava caves in the area, and the stranger was unable to find the right one in spite of the map. He gave up the search and went home empty-handed.

Today, somewhere in a small lava cave along the old stagecoach trail, two large gold bars from the Custer Mine may lie waiting to be discovered.

Illinois
Cave In Rock Treasure

The treasure: Pirate loot and other treasures
Where it is: Along the west bank of the Ohio River in southeastern Illinois

In 1798, land west of the Ohio River was still largely ungoverned and unsettled by pioneers. Gangs of river pirates regularly robbed flatboat travelers and commercial boats traveling on the Ohio River.

A notorious limestone cave in a cliff on the west bank of the Ohio River was once a hideout for these river pirates. This cave, known as Cave In Rock, was a perfect lookout point. It was a huge, vaulted cavern that gave pirates an excellent view up and down the river. This made it easy to watch for unsuspecting travelers who the pirates could rob.

When Abraham Lincoln was just nineteen, his flatboat loaded with farm produce was attacked by pirates on the Ohio River. He was lucky. He escaped with minor injuries. The heartless river pirates sometimes murdered those they robbed and weighted their bodies so that they would sink to the bottom of the river. Often no one ever found out what had happened to the missing travelers.

One of these river pirates, a man named Wilson, opened a shabby tavern at Cave In Rock. He advertised liquor and entertainment. But unlucky river travelers who stopped at Wilson's cave were often robbed and killed.

Brothers Wiley and Micajah Harpe were two of the worst outlaws ever to hide out at Cave In Rock. The bloodthirsty Harpe brothers were so horrible that even the other pirates couldn't stand their evil ways. They once killed a man just for snoring too loudly. After the Harpe brothers pushed a man and his horse over a cliff for fun, the other outlaws had finally had enough. They banished the Harpes from Cave In Rock.

Pirates James Ford and Billy Potts often attacked ferry travelers on the Ohio River near Cave In Rock. It is believed that river pirates named Sam Mason, John Murrell, and Jack Sturdevant also used the cave as a base.

With so much robbing taking place along the Ohio River, many treasure hunters believe a lot of treasure lies buried in the area near Cave In Rock.

Today, Cave In Rock is part of an Illinois state park.

Indiana
The Great Train Robbery Treasure

The treasure: About $98,000 in gold and silver coins, plus cash and bonds

Where it is: Between Seymour and Rockford, in Jackson County, Indiana

On October 6, 1866, the Reno gang made history when they staged the first train robbery in America. The members of the Reno gang, John Reno, Simeon Reno, and Frank Sparks, boarded the eastbound Ohio and Mississippi Railroad express train at Seymour, Indiana. They forced their way into the car carrying treasure and punched out the guard. But they quickly realized they had made a mistake: Only the guard knew the combination to the safe containing the cash, and he was no help. They had knocked him unconscious. The gang shot and hammered the safe, but were unable to open it. However, they still managed to steal ten thousand dollars that wasn't in the safe.

A different train was robbed by two other outlaws just a few months later. When the Reno gang heard about this, they were annoyed that someone had stolen their idea. The gang hunted down the copycats, stole their train loot, and then turned them into the sheriff.

On May 22, 1868, the Reno gang amazed the entire country again. They robbed the Marshfield express train in a new and surprising way. By this time, the Reno gang also included Frank and Bill Reno, as well as another man, who was a safecracker.

When the Marshfield train stopped for wood and water at a water tank, the Reno gang attacked. They knocked out the train engineers and firemen. Next they did something no robbers had tried before. They disconnected two train cars—the train engine and the car carrying the money—from the rest of the train. They took off down the track in those two cars, and left the rest of the train behind blocking the tracks! The gang stopped their two stolen cars a few miles farther down the track, where one of their gang members waited with getaway horses.

Luckily for the gang, the train's treasure was stored in three small boxes. The boxes were much easier to carry than one large safe would have been. The gang packed the boxes on their horses and rode toward Seymour. But they grew worried that a posse might be chasing them. Near midnight, the gang decided to bury the loot somewhere between the towns of Rockford and Seymour. The Reno gang then split up, hoping to lie low for a while.

Americans were shocked by the Reno gang's train robberies. Other gangs soon tried to copy them, staging train hold-ups of their own. But the Reno gang never profited from their unusual robbery of the Marshfield express train. They were all captured or killed before they could return for the treasure. Some were killed by a lynch mob and others were killed in shoot-outs. The Reno gang's ill-gotten train treasure probably still lies where they buried it.

Iowa
The Hidden Fortune on Kelly's Bluff

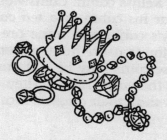

The treasure: Between $50,000 and $100,000 in gold coins

Where it is: Downtown in the city of Dubuque, above Second and Bluff Streets

By the 1830s, a man named Tom Kelly had made a small fortune from his lead mine in Dubuque, Iowa. Like many miners of his time, Kelly didn't trust banks. He hid his money in cans and jars, which he buried on his property.

When a boat carrying one of Kelly's lead shipments sank in 1847, he traveled to New York to try to collect insurance on the lost cargo. While in New York City, he killed a man he thought was trying to rob him. Though he was wealthy, Tom Kelly had always dressed in ragged old clothes and acted unfriendly. His odd clothing and behavior made New York police think that he was insane. There was no trial, but years went by before Kelly was released and allowed to leave New York. He eventually returned to his home in Dubuque, where he died in 1859.

Over time, some of Kelly's hidden treasures have been found. A young boy found $1,800 in gold coins in a tin can at Kelly's cabin. Coins worth $1,500 were also found near his cabin in a tea canister. Legends that Tom Kelly's cabin and mine are haunted have done little to stop treasure hunters from searching for his coins. These coins may be collectors' items, since they are from the early 1800's. They could be worth far more today than their original face value.

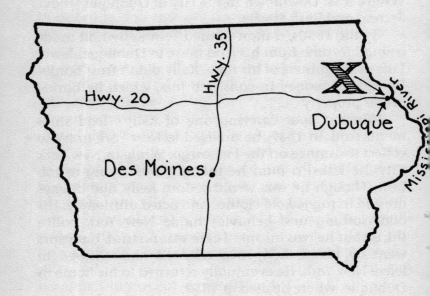

Kansas
Notorious Bill Doolin's Buried Treasure

The treasure: Between $80,000 and $175,000 worth of stolen loot

Where it is: In the hills surrounding Burden, Kansas

Blue-eyed bandit Bill Doolin was one of the most successful outlaws of his day. Doolin rode with the Dalton outlaw gang until 1892, when most of them were killed as they foolishly tried to rob two banks at once. Afterward, Bill Doolin started his own gang and began a crime spree that lasted for the next four years. The Doolin gang robbed banks and trains in Kansas, Texas, Arkansas, Missouri, and Oklahoma, and Doolin soon became notorious.

In 1894, Doolin married a minister's daughter, and they had a son. He used the false name Will Burton and lived with his new family in a house in Burden, Kansas. But he did not stop being a criminal. His gang robbed bank after bank. While other members of the gang spent their loot quickly, Doolin saved his.

In 1896, Marshal William Tilghman captured

Doolin as the outlaw sat in a hot mineral bath at Eureka Springs, Arkansas. The marshal took him by train to a jail in Guthrie, Oklahoma. By now, Doolin was so famous that thousands of people gathered to watch him arrive at the train depot.

However, Doolin wasn't in jail for long. He had a sneaky escape plan in mind. Doolin told the jail

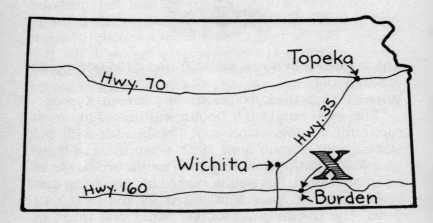

guard that he had buried his outlaw loot near his home in the town of Burden, Kansas. Now that he had been captured, he was going to be in jail a long time. He could not get the money himself, so he promised to let the guard have it. Doolin said that he would draw a map to show him where the treasure was. It was a trick. When the guard came close to give Doolin paper and a pencil, Doolin attacked him and escaped from the jail.

But lawmen were on his trail again in no time. Marshal Heck Thomas soon learned that Doolin's wife and son were in Lawton, Oklahoma, with Doolin's father. On a hunch, Thomas traveled to Lawton and began keeping an eye on Doolin's wife. His hunch paid off. Several days later, Bill Doolin rode into town to visit his family. Thomas killed Doolin in a gunfight.

Doolin's wife told authorities that her husband had in fact buried his stolen loot near their home in Burden. But he had never told her exactly where it was, so no one was able to find it after his death. It is quite possible that infamous outlaw Bill Doolin's treasure still lies buried near the small town of Burden, Kansas.

Kentucky
The Treasure of Morgan's Raiders

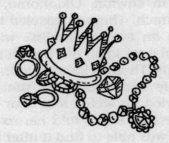

The treasure: About $1 million' worth of gold, silver, and cash (Confederate as well as Union)

Where it is: Along Morgan's path, through Kentucky, from Burkesville in the south to Brandenburg in the north

During the Civil War, Confederate General John Hunt Morgan led 2,500 soldiers on a series of successful raids through Kentucky, Indiana, and Ohio. Under orders from Confederate General Braxton Bragg, Morgan and his raiders first marched from Tennessee into Kentucky on July 2, 1863. General Bragg hoped that this action would draw Union army troops under General William S. Rosecrans's command away from Confederate troops in Tennessee.

Confederate forces were in desperate need of supplies and money at this point in the war. On their path through Kentucky, Morgan and his army looted towns, businesses, and farms. They raided the cities of Salem and Versailles, and were soon carrying a fortune in treasure on their packhorses. But they seemed in no hurry to send it to the Confederate army.

Next, Morgan crossed into Ohio and was captured there on July 26, 1863. But none of his loot could be found. Since he had not had a chance to send the treasure to the Confederate army, many people think he must have hidden it. He and his soldiers were unable to carry much loot or to send it home as they marched. They may have buried it along their path for safekeeping, hoping to come back for it after the war.

Morgan escaped from jail in November 1863. He continued raiding until his army was defeated in Kentucky in June 1864. He was killed in September 1864, during a battle with Union troops. No one knows how much treasure may have been hidden along the trail by Morgan and his raiders, or exactly where it may be.

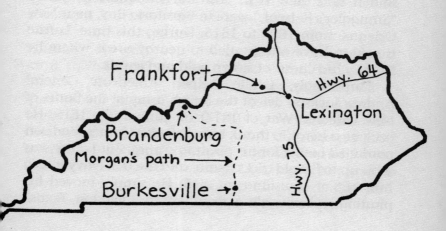

Louisiana
Jean Lafitte's Pirate Booty

The treasure: Pirate treasure worth from $10 million to $100 million

Where it is: Louisiana coast

From 1809 to 1820, French pirate Jean Lafitte robbed ships in the Gulf of Mexico and the Caribbean Sea. He and his pirate band smuggled much of their stolen booty into New Orleans, Louisiana, where they sold it and grew rich. Lafitte's headquarters, called "Smuggler's Retreat," were in Barataria Bay, near New Orleans, from 1809 to 1816. During this time, Lafitte is said to have often sailed to nearby areas where he secretly hid chests of stolen gold and jewels.

Surprisingly, Lafitte helped American General Andrew Jackson defeat the British army at the Battle of New Orleans (War of 1812) on January 8, 1815. He became a hero. To thank him, President James Madison pardoned Lafitte for his pirating crimes. But Lafitte was soon up to his old tricks again, and the U.S. Navy forced him out of Louisiana in 1816. He simply moved his pirating and smuggling operations to Galveston, Texas.

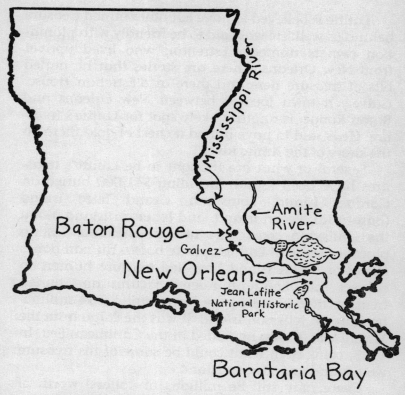

Baton Rouge → •
Galvez •

Amite ←
River

New Orleans →

Jean Lafitte
National Historic
Park

Barataria Bay ↑

Mississippi River

In 1820, Lafitte had to escape from his Galveston empire in a hurry. The U.S. Navy was after him again. He loaded $10 million' worth of treasure onto his ship, the *Pride,* and sailed away. He was never seen again.

What happened to Lafitte and the treasure on his ship? Some people believe he buried it. They think he planned to return for his loot after the navy backed off, but was killed before he could.

Lafitte is believed to have left other buried treasure behind as well. He was said to be friendly with plantation owners named d'Estrehan, who lived upriver from New Orleans. There are stories that he buried bits of treasure here and there at d'Estrehan House. Galvez, a town located between New Orleans and Baton Rouge, is another likely spot for Lafitte's treasure. He is said to have buried a chest of gold there on the shore of the Amite River.

Several of what are thought to be Lafitte's treasures have been found, including $41,000 buried on Gardner Island, Louisiana. Grand Terre Island (Barataria), Pecan Island, and Jefferson Island along the Louisiana coast may also be the final resting places of some of Lafitte's pirate booty. Human bones found at Pecan Island have led treasure hunters to suspect that Lafitte murdered victims and buried treasure there. Lafitte may have buried a $4 million' treasure on Jefferson Island. It was the cargo from the *Santa Elena,* a ship he raided in the Caribbean Sea. In 1923, coins from what could be some of his treasure were found on Jefferson Island.

There may still be millions of dollars' worth of Lafitte's treasure buried in different locations along the coasts of Louisiana and nearby states. Some treasure hunters think Lafitte's ghost is guarding his treasures, so they are too scared to look for them. The exact locations of this pirate's buried treasures remain a mystery.

Maine
Pirate Sam Bellamy's Lost City of Gold

The treasure: Pirate loot of gold, silver coins, and jewels, which some estimate could be worth millions
Where it is: Along Machias Bay, near Highway 1-A

In July 1715, eleven Spanish treasure ships were wrecked in a hurricane along the Florida coast. This disaster attracted many treasure hunters, including an Englishman named Sam Bellamy, who was living in Rhode Island. He and a friend sailed to Florida in 1716, hoping to get rich quick by recovering some of the lost treasure. But by the time they arrived, much of the treasure had already been found.

So Bellamy and his friend decided on another shortcut to becoming rich: They became pirates. The two men joined a pirate ship, and Bellamy quickly became the ship's captain. The pirates spent months attacking ships and capturing valuable cargos.

Bellamy then headed for the coast of Maine, where he built a pine log fort. Some say he called it his "City of Gold." Bellamy continued to plunder ships and may have hidden the stolen cargo at the fort.

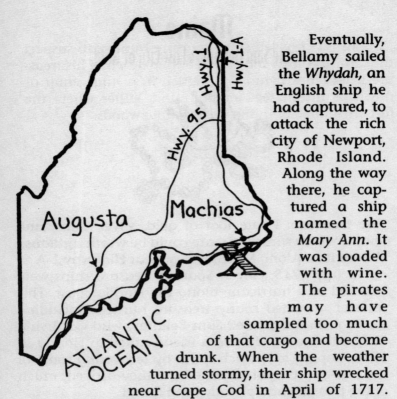

Eventually, Bellamy sailed the *Whydah,* an English ship he had captured, to attack the rich city of Newport, Rhode Island. Along the way there, he captured a ship named the *Mary Ann*. It was loaded with wine. The pirates may have sampled too much of that cargo and become drunk. When the weather turned stormy, their ship wrecked near Cape Cod in April of 1717. Bellamy was killed. Only a few other pirates survived the wreck. Some of those were tried for piracy and hanged. Others were set free because they had been forced into piracy in the first place.

In 1984, a treasure hunter named Barry Clifford salvaged the wreck of Sam Bellamy's pirate ship, the *Whydah*. Many treasure hunters had believed the ship might contain Bellamy's pirate loot, worth as much as $400 million. But Clifford found nowhere near that amount.

This fact has led some treasure hunters to suspect that Sam Bellamy may have buried much of his treasure in his fort. It may be hidden in a huge vault as much as fifteen feet underground, either where the fort once stood or in the surrounding woods.

Maryland
Murder at Treasure Inn

The treasure: Rare gold coins worth about $100,000
Where it is: Reliance, Maryland

Patty Cannon was a gypsy and a slave trader, who owned an inn on two acres in Reliance, Maryland. She and her husband captured slaves escaping from nearby Southern states, such as Virginia and the Carolinas, and sold them for a tidy profit. But they didn't always deliver the slaves to buyers as promised. Between 1819 and 1829, Patty Cannon and her husband are believed to have robbed and killed many men who visited them hoping to buy slaves. The Cannons buried much of the money they stole for safekeeping. They sold the dead men's horses to get rid of any evidence.

One day, a man with the last name Harris arrived at the Cannon's inn asking to buy eight slaves. Patty liked Harris and decided to sell slaves to him instead of killing and robbing him. But Patty's husband had other ideas. Harris could only take four slaves at a time back to his waiting boat. When he took the first

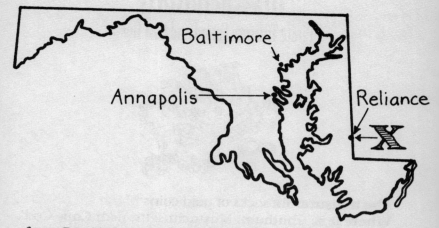

four, Patty's husband followed him, killed him, and stole his money.

Patty was furious when she found out what her husband had done. The next morning, she added a special ingredient to her husband's breakfast: poison! Her husband quickly fell dead. Meanwhile, the four slaves Harris had taken to his ship had escaped. They were picked up by authorities in Delaware. The slaves told them that Patty's husband had killed Harris. When the officers arrived at Patty's cabin, her son broke down and told them everything. Patty poisoned herself before she could be put on trial for any murders.

A little over $7,500' worth of coins has been found on the site of Patty Cannon's inn. The value of her remaining buried treasure is believed to be around $100,000. It could be worth far more if her coins turn out to be rare and collectible.

Massachusetts
Pirate Treasure Found and Lost Again

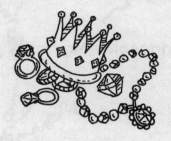

The treasure: Six sacks of gold coins
Where it is: Chatham, Massachusetts, near Cape Cod

One night in 1831, a fisherman named Arthur Doane accidentally struck it rich. He was returning to his ship after visiting a friend on shore when he stumbled upon pirates! They were burying a chest in the sand of North Chatham Beach by lantern light. Doane hid and watched. After the pirates left, he went to discover what they had buried. Grabbing a piece of wood lying on the beach, he dug deep into the sand. Doane could hardly believe his luck: He found a chest filled with twenty-four bags of Spanish gold coins!

Doane decided to hide the treasure so the pirates couldn't find it again. The chest was too heavy to carry far. He took all of the bags out and dragged the empty chest four hundred yards away to a large sand dune. Then he carried the coin-filled bags to the dune, one by one, and refilled the chest. Doane only took one bag of coins for himself. They were heavy, and he knew that he could come back any time for more. He buried the chest eight feet deep in the sand dune and went home.

For many years thereafter, Doane sold a few of his coins at a time to live on. He never told a soul about the treasure until he became ill. Doane thought he might die and did not want the secret treasure to be lost forever. He told a friend named John Eldridge about it. He showed Eldridge some of the coins to prove that he was telling the truth.

The next day, Eldridge located the buried treasure chest right where Doane had told him it would be. He took one bag full of coins, and reburied the chest. Soon afterward, Doane died. Before Eldridge could return for more coins, a storm washed away the sand dune where the chest had been buried. He searched repeatedly along the beach, but never found the chest or the coins again.

Eldridge said that six large bags of coins remained in the chest when it disappeared. These fabulous gold coins may still lie beneath the sands of Chatham Beach in Cape Cod today.

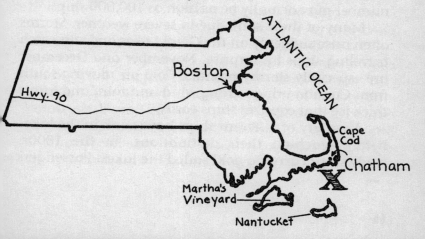

Michigan
Shipwreck Treasure of the Great Lakes

The treasure: Sunken ships' cargos, including silver, gold, copper, and other valuables
Where it is: Great Lakes Erie, Huron, Michigan, and Superior

Michigan is bordered by four of the five Great Lakes: Lake Erie, Lake Huron, Lake Michigan, and Lake Superior. The Great Lakes Shipwreck Historical Museum at Whitefish Point, Michigan, documents 6,000 ships that have wrecked in the Great Lakes since the 1600s. Some treasure hunters believe that the number may actually be as high as 100,000 ships.

Many of these sank due to severe weather. Storms often arise suddenly on the Great Lakes and can catch traveling ships by surprise. November and December are especially stormy months. Cold air moving south from Canada brings strong wind and rain, and forms thick ice that capsizes ships easily.

A variety of different ships have sunk in the lakes before reaching their destinations. In the 1800s, trade ships carrying gold sailed the lakes. Passengers

LAKE SUPERIOR

Grand Island

Great Lakes
Shipwreck
Historical Museum

LAKE HURON

Upper
Peninsula

LAKE MICHIGAN

Alpena

Lansing

Detroit

LAKE ERIE

St. Joseph

traveling on immigrant ships gave their valuables to the captain to be stored in the ship's safe during the voyage. Supply ships bound for pioneer settlements regularly crossed the lakes. In the War of 1812, British and American ships sometimes went down during battles or storms. Ships carrying valuable military supplies, including copper and iron, wrecked in the lakes during both World Wars.

The Great Lakes are freshwater and are extremely cold. These water conditions help preserve sunken treasures better than warm saltwater oceans do. But the cold water temperature and great depths of some of the lakes also make recovery of treasures difficult. Lake Superior is 1,330 feet deep, Lake Michigan is 923 feet deep, and Lake Huron is 750 feet deep. Lake Erie is much shallower at only 210 feet deep.

Some of the treasure ships that have sunk in the Great Lakes near Michigan over the years are:

The *Lexington,* which sank several miles from Pointe Moullie, in Lake Erie, in 1846. This American steamer's cargo included gold valued somewhere between $70,000 and $300,000.

The steamship *Pewabic,* which sank in 1865 when it hit another ship near Alpena, Michigan, in Lake Huron's Thunder Bay. The ship's cargo included gold worth about $1 million, and copper valued at about $700,000.

The *Superior,* which sank near Grand Island, Michigan, in Lake Superior, in 1856. The cargo included $40,000' worth of gold and silver hidden in the safe.

The *Keystone State,* which sank in 1861 northeast of Port Austin in Lake Huron. Its cargo included gold worth about $600,000.

The *R. G. Coburn,* which sank near Harbor Beach, Michigan, in Lake Huron, in 1871. It carried a cargo that included copper valued at $75,000, and gold worth over $100,000.

The *Smith More,* which sank five miles east of Grand Island, Michigan, in Lake Superior, in 1889. Its cargo included 150 barrels of silver ore, and 350 whiskey kegs.

The American steamer *Chicora,* which sank about nine miles southwest of Saint Joseph, Michigan, on Lake Michigan, in 1895. Its cargo included silver ingots, about $50,000 in gold coins, and whiskey. Gold coins that sometimes wash up on nearby Bridgman Beach are thought to be from this shipwreck.

The *Clarion,* which sank about seven miles southeast of Pointe Moullie, Michigan, in Lake Erie, in 1918. Its cargo included gold, silver, and train locomotives.

Minnesota
"Ma" Barker's Gangster Loot

The treasure: Thousands to millions of dollars in bank robbery and kidnapping loot

Where it is: Near Saint Paul, Minnesota

Some people say "Ma" Barker was the mastermind behind the Barker outlaw gang that terrorized the Midwestern United States from 1931 to 1935. Others say she was simply a hillbilly mother who was used as a cover by her four criminal sons.

"Ma" Barker's real name was Arizona Clark. She was born in 1872 and grew up on a poor farm near Springfield, Missouri. In 1892, she married a farmer named George Barker. She changed her name to Kate Barker and had four sons between 1893 and 1903. Her sons, Herman, Lloyd, Arthur (Doc), and Fred, were mischief-makers and thieves. When police and neighbors complained about the boys' behavior, "Ma" Barker thought they were lying. Every time her sons were arrested, she shouted and cried until the police let them go. She thought her boys were wonderful.

After "Ma" Barker's oldest son, Herman, was

arrested for stealing, the family moved to Tulsa, Oklahoma, around 1915. In 1927, Herman was killed in a shoot-out in Kansas. The three remaining Barker boys led lives of crime that landed them in jail more than once during the 1920s. Fred and Doc Barker got out of jail in the early 1930s. They, "Ma," and a young criminal named Alvin Karpis immediately went on a crime spree. The gang began robbing banks throughout the Midwest. By the end of 1933, the Barker-Karpis gang had stolen $3 million' in just three years.

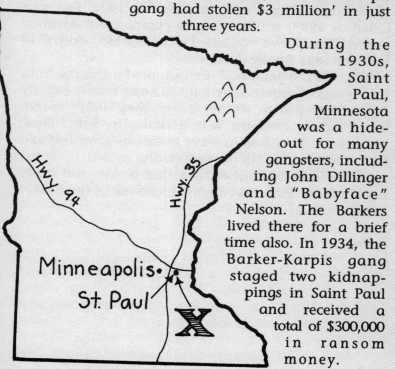

During the 1930s, Saint Paul, Minnesota was a hideout for many gangsters, including John Dillinger and "Babyface" Nelson. The Barkers lived there for a brief time also. In 1934, the Barker-Karpis gang staged two kidnappings in Saint Paul and received a total of $300,000 in ransom money.

By 1934, gang activity across the United States resulted in a series of national crime bills being signed into law by President Franklin D. Roosevelt. These laws gave the FBI better ability to track down outlaw gangs such as the Barker-Karpis gang. J. Edgar Hoover, the head of the FBI, listed the Barkers on the most-wanted list of public enemies.

"Ma" Barker and her youngest son, Fred, were killed in a bloody shoot-out with the FBI in Florida in 1935. Alvin Karpis went to prison in 1936. Doc was killed in 1939, while trying to escape from Alcatraz prison. Once Lloyd was killed in 1949, "Ma" and all of her sons were finally dead.

The Barker gang had accumulated a fortune from their years of criminal activity. No one knows exactly what happened to whatever loot they didn't spend. One of their hideouts was a house in Saint Paul, Minnesota. They had to leave there one morning in a hurry when the FBI unexpectedly raided it. Some treasure hunters believe that this house and other sites in Saint Paul may be the locations of the Barker gang's leftover loot.

Mississippi
Outlaw Treasure in the Devil's Punchbowl

The treasure: Gold and silver bandit loot
Where it is: The Devil's Punchbowl and the Natchez Trace, near Natchez, Mississippi

Just north of Natchez, Mississippi, is a large crater called the Devil's Punchbowl. This crater may be the result of a meteorite hitting Earth in ancient times. Many bandits and outlaws are rumored to have buried treasure in this area.

One of the most interesting of these outlaws was a well-educated man from Virginia named Sam Mason. No one is sure what made Mason turn into an outlaw. For many years he was an honest man. But around 1799, he became the leader of a gang of outlaws at Cave In Rock, along the Ohio River, in Illinois.

As leader, Mason expanded the gang's activities beyond robbing river travelers. They began robbing travelers crossing over land on the southern end of the Natchez Trace. The Natchez Trace was an early road that went all the way from Natchez, Mississippi, to Nashville, Tennessee, a distance of 440 miles. Many people sailed south on the Ohio and Mississippi Rivers to sell their goods in New Orleans, Louisiana. It was not possible to return north again via these rivers in their crude flatboats, since the rivers' currents flowed south. After receiving payment for their goods in New Orleans, travelers often returned northward on foot by way of the Natchez Trace. With their pockets full of riches, they were easy prey for Mason and his gang.

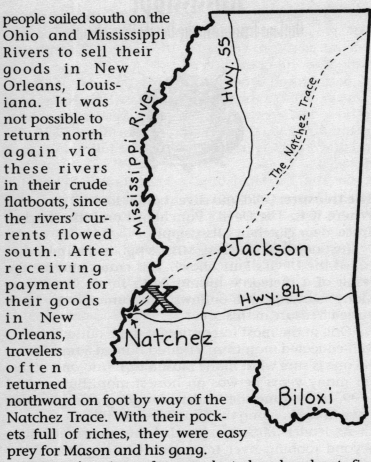

Mason's reign of terror lasted only about five years. A reward was placed on his head, and a notoriously evil outlaw named Wiley Harpe killed him in 1804 to claim it. However, Harpe's idea backfired when he delivered Mason's head to the sheriff in Natchez as proof that he had killed him. Harpe was recognized as a wanted outlaw himself, and was hanged for his crimes.

Sam Mason is believed to have buried at least one large treasure at the Devil's Punchbowl. He is also said to have hidden treasures in other Mississippi towns, including $250,000 near a tavern in Bissell; $75,000 in Little Sand Creek; and an iron pot full of loot near Natchez.

In 1927, a Mississippi farmer named Robert (or Reber) Dove discovered an iron pot on his farm. It was a huge pot almost seven feet by four feet. He had heard the tale of Mason's iron pot full of treasure, and believed he had found it. Dove dug excitedly for the pot, but the quicksandlike, muddy soil just pulled the pot deeper underground. He was unable to grab it. This pot's location is known, and others have since tried to retrieve it. But no one has managed to do it yet.

Missouri
Where Gold Grows on Trees

The treasure: A fortune in gold coins
Where it is: Near Reeds Spring, in the Ozark Mountains in southwest Missouri

For years after his arrival in the Missouri Ozarks around 1830, a man with the last name Keith hunted, trapped, and did odd jobs to earn a living. He also preached at church services, got married, and built a small cabin.

Then the 1849 gold rush lured Keith to California in search of gold. He was lucky! He struck it rich and returned home with two mules carrying sacks full of gold coins. The entire town soon learned of his new-found wealth. Some were jealous. Keith began to worry that someone would try to steal his gold. He spent many nights guarding it with a rifle.

Eventually, Keith decided the gold wasn't safe. He loaded it onto his mules and took it through the woods to a hiding place. Keith never told his family where he had hidden his treasure. But they later reported that it took only an hour for him to leave the cabin and bury his gold. Therefore, the gold may not have been hidden very far from his home.

Keith once told someone that he was building a treasure room. He said that he had put a casket inside it, and that he planned to go to this room when he was ready to die. Could his treasure room have been located inside one of many limestone caves in the Ozark Mountains? At one time he was seen moving rocks that he could have used to disguise such a cave's entrance.

Another possibility is that Keith buried the gold in his favorite orchard. He sometimes said that when he needed money, he just went to his orchard, where the gold grew on trees.

One day, Keith disappeared into the woods with his rifle and never returned. The body of a man holding a rifle was discovered in an orchard four miles away from Keith's home, months later. Perhaps this old orchard was the location of his treasure rather than the orchard on his property, as some had thought.

The true location of Keith's treasure remains unknown. Perhaps somewhere, in a cave or an orchard, there is a secret room full of gold coins that still holds Keith's empty casket.

Montana
Gold Near Custer's Last Stand

The treasure: Gold worth $375,000
Where it is: On the shores of the Bighorn River, in Montana, near the site of General Custer's famous battle

On June 25, 1876, American General George Custer and his army were killed in a battle with the Sioux and Cheyenne tribes near the Little Bighorn River. On that same day, Captain Grant Marsh was sailing a steamboat called the *Far West* along the nearby Bighorn River. The *Far West* carried supplies and mail, which Marsh planned to deliver to General Alfred Terry. Terry was the commander of all American troops in the area, and his mission was to relocate the Indians onto reservations.

Most researchers agree that the *Far West* was carrying a shipment of gold. Many think that the gold was an army payroll shipment worth as much as $375,000. However, it is not clear how the *Far West* came to have this gold onboard. The story goes that a wagon driver named Gil Longworth accidently met the *Far West* on June 26, and begged Captain Marsh to take the army gold onboard. Longworth was afraid of the Indians in the area and wanted to return home. Captain Marsh agreed to take the gold and drop it off at its destination at Bismarck, North Dakota.

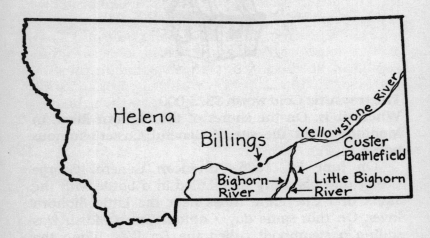

However, Captain Marsh quickly learned of Custer's battle disaster and worried that his boat might be attacked by the Indians. He could see their campfires all along the river shores as he passed. Just in case, Marsh decided to hide the gold on the shore of the Bighorn River to prevent it from being sunk or stolen. One report says that he and his men buried it in a small cave on a pine ridge along the Bighorn River, about twenty miles upstream from the mouth of the Little Bighorn River. Another report says it was buried on the shore of the Bighorn River near the

Yellowstone River instead. Either way, it probably wasn't buried far inland. It only took Marsh and his men about four hours to row ashore one night, bury the gold, and return to the *Far West*.

All of General Custer's approximately 250 soldiers and officers had been killed in the Little Bighorn battle. But there were other army troops fighting the Sioux and Cheyenne in the area at this time also. The *Far West* helped carry many wounded soldiers to the hospital in Bismarck. The danger of Indian attacks prevented Captain Marsh or anyone else from returning for the gold for some time. Meanwhile, heavy rains caused mud slides along the river shores. A search was eventually made, but the gold could never be found again.

Nebraska
Duke Sherman's Unlucky Gold Train

The treasure: $60,000' worth of gold
Where it is: Buried near Staplehurst, Nebraska

Seventeen-year-old Duke Sherman was bored with his job at a stockyard in Omaha, Nebraska. He dreamed of being wealthy enough to enjoy life without working. Sherman thought it was his lucky day when he heard about a gold shipment worth $60,000. The gold would be leaving Omaha on a train headed for Lincoln, Nebraska, the very next morning. Sherman had never robbed anyone before. But he thought if outlaws could do it, why couldn't he?

That night, Sherman stole a horse and wagon and followed the train tracks partway to Lincoln. About ten miles outside of Lincoln, he stopped to wait for the train. The next morning, he watched as the train approached and stopped nearby so cattle could cross the tracks. Sherman left his wagon hidden in the bushes, ran to the train, and pointed a gun at the engineer. The frightened engineer and treasure guard gave him the metal boxes full of gold coins, and

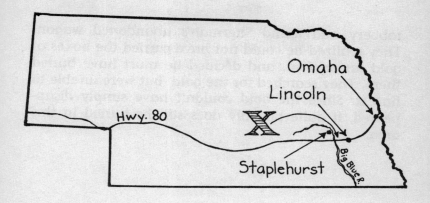

Sherman told them to continue on to Lincoln. As the train took off, Sherman loaded the heavy boxes of gold onto his wagon. Little did he know that he had been spotted stealing the horse and wagon back in Omaha the night before. A posse was already chasing him.

The gold was far heavier than Sherman had thought it would be. He had only traveled about twelve miles when his horse began limping. They could go no farther. He unloaded the boxes and buried them, so no one could take them while he was gone. Then he walked to a nearby farm and tried to steal a new horse. The farmer caught him in the act of trying to saddle one of his horses. When Sherman fired his gun, the farmer shot back and killed him. As he lay dying, Sherman tried to tell the farmer about the buried gold. But the farmer couldn't understand him.

Meanwhile, the Omaha posse learned of the train

robbery and found Sherman's abandoned wagon. They realized he could not have carried the boxes of gold far on foot, and decided he must have buried them. They searched for the gold, but were unable to find it. Since the gold couldn't have simply disappeared, it quite possibly does still lie buried in this area.

Nevada
The Lost Silver Bullet Mine

The treasure: Silver ore
Where it is: Black Rock Desert, in northwestern Nevada

James Allen Hardin left his home in Missouri in 1849 and joined a pioneer wagon train headed for California. The wagons had traveled for many weeks by the time they reached Nevada's Black Rock Desert and decided to rest for a few days near Pahute Peak and Mud Meadows River. Hardin and another man used the break to go hunting, since they were low on food. They rode into the nearby Black Rock Mountain Range, but were unable to find any game.

On the way back to camp, the two men rode a few miles north of Double Hot Springs. They crossed a stream that had been caused by recent rains. Hardin noticed pieces of shiny metal scattered in the stream and in the rocks nearby. It looked like lead, and he hoped that he could use it to make bullets. He collected pieces of the metal, and they returned to camp.

That very night, Hardin tested the metal. It was soft

and easy to mold. He made bullets out of most of it, and saved the rest to use later.

The wagon train moved on to California, where Hardin settled and eventually became a carpenter in Petaluma. Months passed, and Hardin forgot about the metal he had found in the stream. One day an assayer, who was knowledgeable about rock ore, visited Hardin's shop. He got excited when he saw the metal. To Hardin's surprise, the assayer told him it was high quality silver. Hardin wanted to go back in search of the silver immediately, but he didn't have enough money to go prospecting.

In 1858, Hardin was finally able to organize some prospectors to help him try to relocate the silver. He led them to the area where the wagon train had camped years earlier, but he was unable to find the stream or the silver. The prospectors searched for two years, but were forced to give up in 1860. Paiute Indians were active in the area, making it too dangerous to stay longer.

In the following years, so many prospectors tried to find Hardin's lost silver that a mining town grew up in the Black Rock area. It was called Hardin City, named after James Hardin. Very little silver was ever found, and Hardin City is now a ghost town.

Many treasure seekers believe that Hardin's lost silver is still somewhere in the foothills of the Black Rock Mountains. Perhaps another storm will someday create runoff streams that will uncover the silver once again.

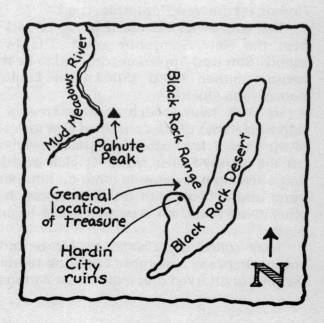

New Hampshire
The Pirate Treasure of John Quelch

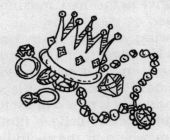

The treasure: Gold and silver pirate plunder worth $100,000 to $1,000,000

Where it is: The Isles of Shoals, near Portsmouth Harbor, off the New Hampshire coast

The Isles of Shoals are a group of rocky islands near the New Hampshire coast. The two largest islands, Star and Appledore, are said to be the sites of treasure buried by a little-known English pirate named John Quelch.

In 1703, John Quelch and the crew of a British ship named the *Charles* mutinied and took command of the ship. They tossed the captain overboard, and left the scene of their crime. Quelch raised a pirate flag, showing a skeleton holding an hourglass in one hand and a heart with an arrow through it in the other. Quelch and his crew were off to begin a life of piracy.

They sailed the *Charles* to Africa and western Europe. Between November 1703 and February 1704, the pirates attacked and looted nine Portuguese ships near Brazil. They captured a wealth of gold dust, gold and silver coins, guns, fabrics, and other goods. Quelch was now a rich man.

In May of 1704, Quelch sailed back to Marblehead, Massachusetts, where he had first stolen the *Charles.* He planned to retire from piracy and enjoy the treasure it is believed he had secretly buried on nearby Star and Appledore Islands off the coast of New Hampshire. He had somehow managed to steer clear of the law so far, and thought his luck would hold. When questioned upon his return, he boldly claimed that he had never even been a pirate. He told everyone that he had been forced to take over the *Charles* only because the ship's captain had already died. Few believed this tale.

After a quick trial in June of 1704, Quelch and some of his crew were found guilty of piracy. Before he was hanged, Quelch made a speech to the crowd that had gathered to watch. He denied to the bitter end that he had ever been a pirate.

A journal believed to have been written by Quelch was found in the late 1700s.

It told of an amazing treasure the pirate had hidden on Star Island. Quelch was reportedly seen burying treasure on Star Island shortly before he and his crew were hanged. However, the journal gave no directions to help find this treasure. Construction workers on the island later accidentally discovered a few gold pieces, which may have been part of Quelch's booty. The rest of this treasure has never been found.

Quelch is also said to have buried gold dust and silver bars on the west side of Appledore Island, which is actually part of the state of Maine. This treasure also remains lost.

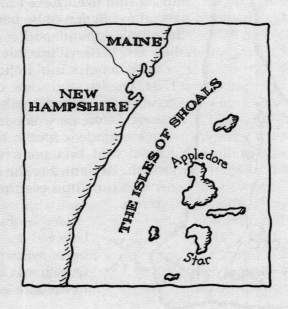

New Jersey
Pine Robber Booty

The treasure: Bandit loot
Where it is: New Jersey's Pine Barrens

During the American Revolution, there was little law enforcement in New Jersey. Gangs of bandits terrorized and robbed the colonists whenever they pleased. These outlaws were nicknamed pine robbers because they hid out in the Pine Barrens, great pine forests in southeastern New Jersey.

Some infamous pine robbers were John Bacon, Richard Bird, and Humphrey Davenport. But just as well known were William Giberson, Joe Mulliner, and their gang. Mulliner liked to go to barn dances, where he would rob merrymakers at gunpoint. His gang also robbed stagecoaches and kidnapped people for ransom money. Altogether, pine robbers may have stolen more than a million dollars in gold, silver, and jewels from 1775 to 1780.

Pine robbers were experts at hiding their stolen treasure in man-made caves, sand dunes, and along streambeds in the Pine Barrens. One of their hideouts

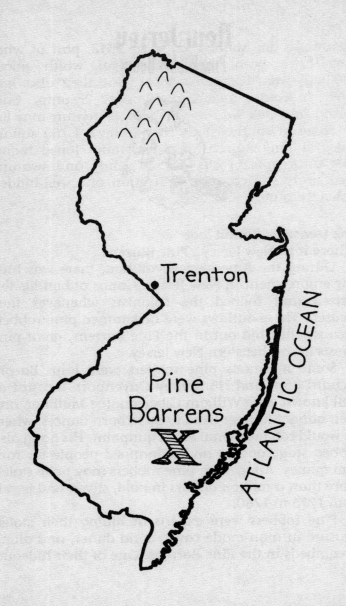

Trenton

Pine
Barrens

X

ATLANTIC OCEAN

was along the Mullica River. In 1847, part of what may have been their loot—silver worth about $30,000—was discovered there. But they also had other hideouts, including Hemlock Swamp, Cold Spring, and Oak Swamp, where more treasure may lie.

Some of southeastern New Jersey's 1,700 square miles of Pine Barrens remains undeveloped today. This thick pine brush with its sandy and swampy areas may still conceal more than one well-hidden stolen treasure.

New Mexico
The Victorio Peak Treasure

The treasure: An estimated $150 million' to $200 billion' worth of gold and other valuables

Where it is: In a cavern in Victorio Peak, near the San Andres Mountains of southern New Mexico, on the U. S. Army's White Sands Missile Range

In November 1937, a man named Milton Noss went deer hunting in the San Andres Mountains of New Mexico. While resting, he noticed strange marks on some rocks outside of a cave in a 490-foot hill in the mountains called Victorio Peak. Noss quickly realized that what he had found was not a cave at all. It was an old mine shaft. A Spanish priest named Father La Rue had mined gold in these mountains in the 1700s. According to legend, he had been killed by either Mexican or Apache raiders and had left his gold behind. Was this one of his mines?

Noss was curious, so he crawled into the long, narrow shaft to investigate. When he came to a small opening in a wall, he wiggled through it. It opened into a large cavern, where he found stacks of black

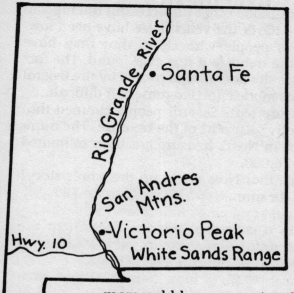

bars as well as religious statues and jewels. Noss scraped the black grime off of a few bars. Underneath, they were solid gold!

Because the bars were heavy, Noss took only one. He may have removed more gold bars, some jewelry, and coins on another visit soon afterward as well. However, Noss told few people about his gold since it was against the law for anyone in the United States to own gold in 1937.

Noss later returned to the cave with dynamite. He blasted the opening, hoping to widen the entrance to the gold-filled room. But the blast caused a rock slide, which collapsed the roof of the tunnel and closed off the room full of gold completely. Although he tried to dig back inside many times, he was unsuccessful. Noss never saw the treasure again.

Milton Noss was killed in 1949 as a result of what may have been an argument about the gold. His family has since made other unsuccessful attempts to get the treasure. Over the years there have been lawsuits by various people who claim that they have some right to the treasure if it is ever found. The fact that the treasure site lies on land owned by the federal government has made efforts to retrieve it difficult.

Is this treasure real? Several people claimed that they had actually seen part of the treasure. The number of gold bars in Noss's treasure has been estimated at as many as 16,000.

Is it possible that Noss made up the whole story? No one knows for sure.

New York
Dutch Schultz's Gangster Loot

The treasure: About $7 million
Where it is: On the shores of the Esopus Creek, in the Catskill Mountains of New York State, near Phoenicia

In 1920, the 18th Amendment was added to the U.S. Constitution. It made illegal the production, sale, and transportation of alcoholic beverages illegal in the United States. The era from 1920 to 1933 was known as "Prohibition" since beer, whiskey, gin, and other alcohol were prohibited. (Prohibition ended in 1933 when the 18th Amendment was repealed.)

Police soon had their hands full trying to stop criminals known as "bootleggers" from illegally making and selling alcohol. Gang wars broke out among the "bootleggers" when they couldn't agree on a division of territory where each could sell alcohol. They also battled each other over scarce supplies needed to make alcohol.

During the Prohibition era, a gangster known as Dutch Schultz went on a crime spree in New York that made him a wealthy man. He successfully bootlegged

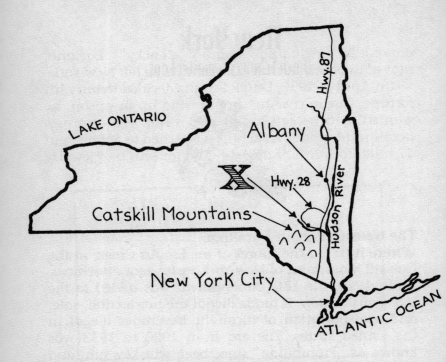

liquor, and soon expanded into the restaurant business and illegal gambling as well. He and his gang members are estimated to have committed as many as 135 murders, using weapons such as ice picks and tommy guns.

In spite of an occasional gang war, business was good for Schultz. But his luck ended in 1933, when he learned he was going to be arrested for federal income tax evasion. Schultz feared that he would be put on trial, found guilty, and imprisoned for not paying taxes, just as gangster Al Capone had recently been. He went into hiding in Bridgeport, Connecticut. Other ganglords, including Charley "Lucky" Luciano, moved in on his territory the minute he left New York.

In April of 1933, Dutch Schultz decided to bury his fortune. Just in case he should wind up in prison, he wanted it to be safe until he got out. His attorney, accountant, and several others watched as Schultz put $7 million' worth of thousand-dollar bills and jewelry

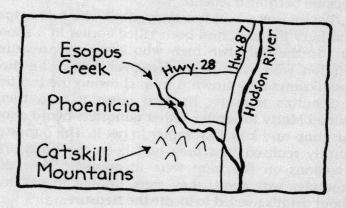

into a steel box. The box was about three feet long and two feet wide. Schultz and his bodyguard, Lulu Rosenkrantz, put the box in the trunk of Schultz's car and drove into the Catskill Mountains. They buried the treasure box there on the banks of Esopus Creek. Schultz planned to reclaim it once he was out of trouble with the law.

Federal agents eventually did catch up with Dutch Schultz, but were unable to convict him of not paying taxes. He had hidden his loot, so there was no proof that he had any taxable wealth. Once the danger of prison passed, Schultz tried to pick up where he had left off and rebuild his empire. But a "contract" had been put out on his life. He was killed by another gangster in October 1935. Schultz didn't die instantly. While in the hospital, he talked endlessly about his fabulous buried treasure. Word leaked out, and his treasure became a legend.

Rosenkrantz, Schultz's bodyguard who had helped him bury the loot, had been killed earlier in a shootout. So the only two men who knew the treasure's location were now dead. However, before he died, Rosenkrantz had drawn a map showing the location of Schultz's treasure. He had given it to a friend named Marty Krompier. Other gangsters heard about this map and killed Krompier to get it. The gangsters quickly realized that they had been too hasty. The directions on the map were incomplete. Now that Krompier was dead, they were unable to ask him about details needed to locate the treasure.

Because eight witnesses saw Dutch Schultz pack up his treasure, many treasure hunters believe this treasure truly exists. As far as anyone knows, none of it has ever turned up. Schultz's steel box full of millions is very likely still where he buried it in the Catskill Mountains.

North Carolina
Blackbeard's Buried Pirate Treasure

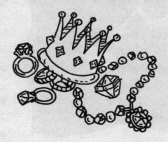

The treasure: Gold and silver coins, jewels, and other pirate booty

Where it is: Ocracoke Island, off the North Carolina coast

Blackbeard, whose real name was probably Edward Teach or Thatch, was one of the most terrifying pirates who ever lived. He enjoyed battle, and murdered men, women, and children alike. Blackbeard was over six feet tall and had a booming voice. His nickname came from his black beard, which hung nearly to his waist. He sometimes braided it with ribbons, or even burning candles! He was trying to look and act so fierce that ships would give up without much of a fight.

Blackbeard attacked trading ships along the Atlantic coast of North America in the early 1700s. He stole their cargos and soon had an incredible fortune. Between battles, Blackbeard often went to the North Carolina coast to relax. He is believed to have had homes in Edenton, Elizabeth City, and Ocracoke, and

Blackbeard's Pirate Flag

may have had as many as fourteen wives!

In 1718, England ruled the east coast of what is now the United States. King George I had grown tired of pirates attacking his ships. He promised to pardon any pirate who would stop pirating immediately, but vowed to kill any who would not. Some pirates agreed to this deal, but Blackbeard refused.

Instead, he went to North Carolina and began to make the king even more annoyed. He started charging an illegal toll to any ship that wanted to enter North Carolina's Ocracoke port. For a time, North Carolina colonists tolerated Blackbeard. The people were poor and were glad to get the merchandise he sold to them at good prices, even if it was stolen. But eventually, the colonists also got tired of his treacherous tricks. Governor Alexander Spotswood of the nearby state of Virginia began plotting Blackbeard's downfall with the help of the English navy.

In November 1718, Lieutenant Robert Maynard of the English navy was sent to put a stop to Blackbeard's piracy. A great sea battle occurred between Blackbeard and Maynard at Ocracoke Inlet, and Blackbeard was killed. He did not die easily. It took twenty stabbings with a sword and five gunshots to finally kill him. To make an example of Blackbeard, Maynard cut off his head and hung it from the yardarm of his ship. The pirate's headless body was thrown into the sea along North Carolina's coast.

There are many tales that Blackbeard buried stolen treasure during his lifetime. Much of his gold and silver may have been buried for safekeeping on Ocracoke Island. Other likely treasure locations in North Carolina include Plum Point and the shores of the Pasquotank River.

But treasure hunters seeking Blackbeard's loot had better not be afraid of ghosts. Some say that the pirate buried a dead body with each treasure, so its ghost would scare treasure hunters away. Blackbeard's ghost is also said to haunt his treasures, and his headless body is rumored to still swim along the North Carolina coast.

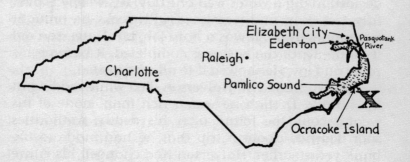

North Dakota
A Well-Hidden Gold Treasure

The treasure: Gold coins worth over $1 million
Where it is: Grand Forks, North Dakota, in Nelson County

Little is known about Gustav Halverson except that he was a wealthy Swedish man who never married and seemed to have no family. He owned a large wheat farm in North Dakota but enjoyed reading the books in his library more than farming. In fact, he did little farmwork at all.

So it surprised everyone when Halverson suddenly decided to dig a water well one day. His well was over fifty feet deep and was lined with rocks he brought from miles away. It was a hard job, but Halverson did it alone. Once the well was completed, it became his pride and joy. He showed it to all who visited.

Many years later, Halverson died while reading in his library. Though he was a rich man, none of his wealth could be found after his death. Authorities soon learned about a trip that he had made to the bank years earlier. Halverson had changed his entire

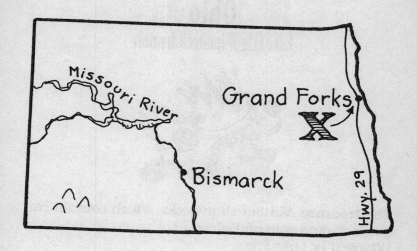

million-dollar fortune into gold coins! It was decided that he must have buried the coins somewhere on his farm. A thorough search of his property took place, but no coins were found.

Many years later, a diary that is believed to have been written by Halverson was found in an old trunk. According to this diary, Halverson hid his gold at the bottom of his well! Unfortunately, both his house and well had been torn down by this time. The search for his treasure was renewed, but without success. Neither his well nor his gold has ever been rediscovered.

Ohio
Lake Erie Shipwreck Treasure

The treasure: Various shipwrecks, which contain cargos including gold and silver

Where it is: Lake Erie

Lake Erie borders Ohio on the north and has been the site of many shipwrecks. It is the shallowest of the five Great Lakes, at 210 feet. Nineteenth-century gold and silver coins have washed up on the shores of Lake Erie about two miles east of Vermilion, Ohio. These are believed to be from a nearby shipwreck.

Some ships known to have sunk in Lake Erie include:

The 40-ton *Griffin,* which went down in a storm in September 1679, and was the first recorded treasure shipwreck on the lake. The *Griffin* reportedly contained army payroll in the form of gold coins.

In 1763 and 1764, British ships sank in Lake Erie near Rocky River, Ohio. A British army officer named Wilkins lost twenty boats carrying supplies in 1763. John Bradstreet, another British officer, lost numerous vessels in 1764. They carried trade goods, weapons, and silverware.

The *G. R. Griffin,* which sank just north of Lorain, Ohio, in 1896, and carried over $500,000' worth of copper.

A ferry named the *Marquette & Bessemer,* which

sank about seven miles east of Conneaut, Ohio, in 1909. Its cargo included about $65,000 in gold and silver, and thirty-seven railroad cars.

An American barge named the *Cleveco*, which sank four miles from Cleveland, Ohio, in 1943. It carried about $80,000' worth of gold and silver.

Airplanes have also crashed into Lake Erie, including a DC-3 carrying $30,000 in cash.

Oklahoma
The Loot of Outlaw Jesse James

The treasure: Gold worth over $2 million
Where it is: Cement, Oklahoma

Jesse James and his brother Frank were outlaws. Their gang robbed banks, trains, and stagecoaches in Texas, Oklahoma, and Missouri beginning around 1866. In 1876, the outlaws staged a robbery in Mexico that earned them a fortune. They ambushed a huge overland shipment of gold bars belonging to a Mexican general. The James gang killed the guards, took the eighteen burros loaded with gold, and headed north to Oklahoma.

They soon began to worry that lawmen would catch them. They couldn't carry the heavy gold without the burros, but the burros made them slow and easy to spot. They decided to hide their loot and come back for it later.

The outlaws dug a hole, put the gold in, and covered it with rocks. They scratched their names on a bucket using a nail, and buried the bucket beside a nearby cottonwood tree. A burro shoe was also left

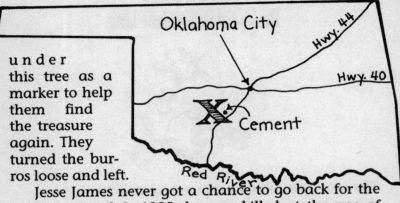

under this tree as a marker to help them find the treasure again. They turned the burros loose and left.

Jesse James never got a chance to go back for the gold. On April 3, 1882, he was killed at the age of thirty-four in Missouri by one of his own gang members, who hoped to collect a reward. After Jesse died, his brother Frank tried to find their treasure. But when he went back to look, the landmarks he remembered were gone. The trees had been cut, farms had been plowed, and homes had been built. Frank looked for many years, but never found the gold.

Years later, someone found the burro shoe beside the stump of a cottonwood tree near Cement, Oklahoma. In 1931, someone also found a bucket with writing and drawings on it. The only words that could still be read said: "On this, the 5 day of March, 1876 . . ." There were also drawings of a burro and an arrow on the bucket. Was this the James gang's bucket? Maybe so, but how far from it and in which direction was the treasure itself buried? No one has figured this out, so the James gang's outlaw loot has never been discovered.

Oregon
Wagon Train Blue Bucket Gold

The treasure: Many gold nuggets
Where it is: A canyon in southeastern Oregon, along the Malheur River

In 1845, a wagon train was traveling west along the Oregon Trail. It included over one hundred wagons with nearly a thousand people, as well as cattle, horses, and other livestock. Some of them split off near what is today the town of Vale, and headed for California.

The rest of the families took a shortcut to Oregon, where many of them hoped to begin farming. This shortcut took them through a rocky and treacherous canyon, which made travel slow. But the families sang songs to pass the time, and the children played in the stream that ran alongside the trail. As they splashed, the children picked up bright stones in the stream. Soon a contest was going to see who could gather the most of the shiny yellow stones. They collected their treasures in the blue buckets many of the wagons carried. Their parents were so busy trying to guide their wagons through the difficult canyon that they paid little attention.

Days later, the wagons reached the rich farming area of Oregon's Willamette River valley. The settlers unpacked and began building homes. The blue buckets

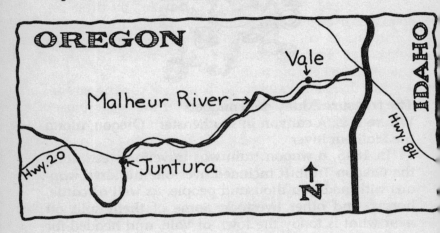

were needed to haul water, so the children's yellow stones were dumped out. Some children kept their prizes, but many of the stones were lost.

Months went by before some California miners passed through the new settlement. When they saw the shiny stones, they were amazed. The stones were actually gold nuggets!

Some people think that this may have been the first gold ever discovered in Oregon. The 1849 California gold rush would not begin for four more years. So the pioneers hadn't considered that their children's stones might be gold when they found them. Some of the settlers tried to go back and find more gold in the canyon, but hostile Paiute Indians stopped them. By the time they were able to return and search, no one could find the gold again.

Over time, the pioneer trail traveled by these settlers was used less and less until it nearly disappeared. Earthquakes and floods have further changed the landscape. Today, no one is sure where the canyon of the blue bucket gold really was.

Are there still gold nuggets in that canyon stream where the children played, just waiting to be picked up? Perhaps!

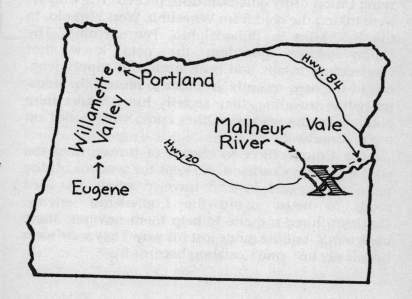

Pennsylvania
Civil War Gold Bars

The treasure: Twenty-eight 50-pound gold bars, worth as much as $8 million altogether

Where it is: Cameron County, north of Highway 80

During the Civil War, in 1863, a wagon train carrying Union army gold bars disappeared. The wagons were taking the gold from Wheeling, West Virginia, to the U.S. Mint in Philadelphia, Pennsylvania. The Union soldiers guarding the gold knew that Confederate troops had been attacking supply wagons in the area recently. In order to protect the treasure while traveling, they secretly hid it under false bottoms in the wagons. Other cargo was loaded on top to disguise it.

The Union officer in charge of transporting the gold was John Castleton. He kept the wagons off the main roads, and instead traveled small, less-used roads to better avoid the Confederate enemy. Castleton hired a guide to help them navigate these back roads, but the guide lost his way. They were soon hopelessly lost, and Castleton became ill.

The Union officers decided to split into two groups. Each went a different direction to try to find help. One group was led by Castleton, and the other was led by a man named Connors. Castleton's group took the gold. Two weeks later, Connors's group returned with help. They found Castleton's wagons, but no men or gold. They had all vanished!

Union army officials suspected that Connors had somehow stolen the gold. But Connors suspected the guide Castleton had hired. Detectives from the Pinkerton National Detective Agency and the U.S. Army investigated. Part of one of the gold bars was found buried under a tree stump. But none of the rest of the gold bars or Castleton and his men were ever located. Some treasure hunters think this gold may be buried in Pennsylvania, near where Castleton was last seen.

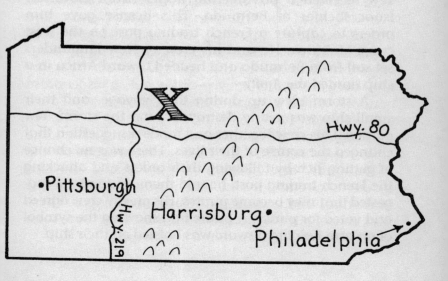

Rhode Island
The Treasure of Pirate Thomas Tew

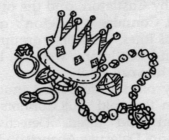

The treasure: $100,000–$200,000 in gold coins
Where it is: Newport, Rhode Island

Thomas Tew was a well-dressed pirate who sported a flowing cape and a long silk scarf. But he didn't start out to be a fashionable pirate. In 1692, Tew received a privateering license from Governor Isaac Richier of Bermuda. This license gave him orders to capture a French trading post on the west coast of Africa. He and his crew of New Englanders set sail from Bermuda and headed toward Africa in a ship named the *Amity*.

A storm blew up during their voyage, and their small ship was nearly destroyed. After the storm, Tew gathered his crew together and made a suggestion that changed the course of their lives. There was no chance of getting rich by following their orders and attacking the French trading post, he told them. Instead, he suggested that they become pirates. His greedy crew agreed and voted for piracy. A pirate flag showing the symbol of an arm holding a sword was hoisted on their ship.

Thomas Tew's Pirate Flag

They sailed the *Amity* around the Cape of Good Hope at the southern tip of Africa and then headed north toward the Red Sea. The pirates soon found the adventure and wealth they were seeking. Their first successful attack was against an Arabian ship loaded with gold and jewels. After a year or so of pirating, Tew became a wealthy man.

But Tew eventually grew homesick. In December 1693, he decided to take his share of pirate treasure and go back to his home in Newport, Rhode Island.

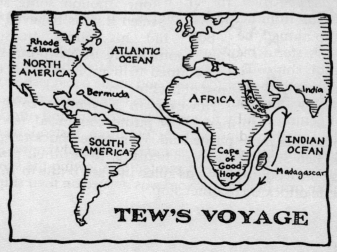

TEW'S VOYAGE

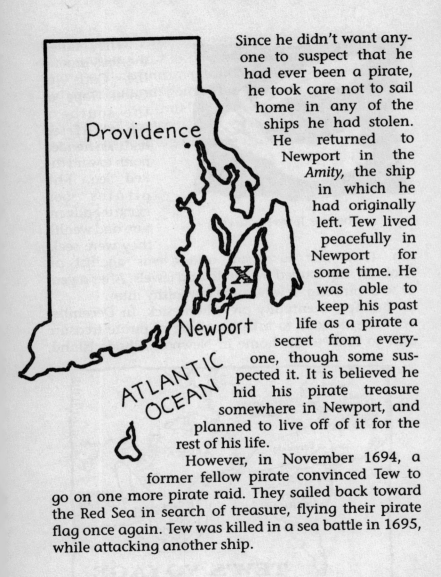

Providence

Newport

ATLANTIC OCEAN

Since he didn't want anyone to suspect that he had ever been a pirate, he took care not to sail home in any of the ships he had stolen. He returned to Newport in the *Amity*, the ship in which he had originally left. Tew lived peacefully in Newport for some time. He was able to keep his past life as a pirate a secret from everyone, though some suspected it. It is believed he hid his pirate treasure somewhere in Newport, and planned to live off of it for the rest of his life.

However, in November 1694, a former fellow pirate convinced Tew to go on one more pirate raid. They sailed back toward the Red Sea in search of treasure, flying their pirate flag once again. Tew was killed in a sea battle in 1695, while attacking another ship.

What became of his treasure? After a fire in 1880, coins were found in the woods surrounding Tew's home. More were found during a construction project in the 1950s. The coins were dated around 1690, and had melted together in the 1880 fire.

Many people believe that most of Tew's pirate treasure still lies buried somewhere near his beloved home in Newport.

South Carolina
Mary Anne Townsend's Pirate Treasure

The treasure: Gold and silver coins, jewels, and artifacts

Where it is: The swampy marshes of South Carolina

Charleston, South Carolina, was a busy shipping port, where cargos arrived daily in the early 1700s. Pirates such as Blackbeard and Stede Bonnet attacked these cargo ships regularly and found the marshes west of Charleston to be a good place to hide stolen booty.

An even more unusual pirate in the Charleston area at this time was a beautiful, red-haired woman named Mary Anne Townsend. Before turning to piracy, Townsend lived in Jamestown, Virginia, and was honest and respected. Her family was wealthy, and her uncle held a government office. But Townsend's life changed when she was unlucky enough to be a passenger on a ship that Blackbeard attacked near Bermuda. Townsend watched as others on the ship were killed or forced to walk the plank by the pirates. She spit at Blackbeard's men when it was

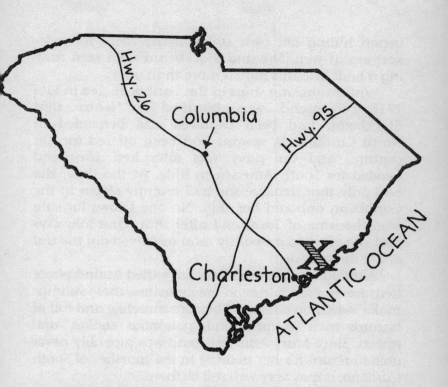

her turn. The minute Blackbeard saw Townsend, he fell under the spell of her beauty. He kidnapped her, gave her jewels and gold, and begged her to join his pirate band. She eventually agreed, and Blackbeard taught her the art of piracy.

Months later, Townsend was captain of her own pirate ship, the *Odyssey*. She plundered ships in the Atlantic Ocean and the Caribbean Sea. Blackbeard showed her a secret place in the South Carolina marsh where he sometimes hid treasure. Townsend began hiding her own stolen booty there for safe-keeping as well. She and Blackbeard were seen rowing a boat into this marsh more than once.

While attacking ships in the Caribbean Sea in late 1718, Townsend was horrified to learn that Blackbeard had been captured and beheaded in North Carolina. A reward had been offered for her capture, and the navy was after her! Townsend headed for South America to hide. At the time, she had only that treasure she had recently stolen in the Caribbean onboard her ship. No one knows for sure what became of Townsend after that. One tale says that she married a wealthy man and lived out the rest of her life in Peru.

Although treasure hunters have tried to find pirate treasures in the Charleston area marshes, these swamps make searching difficult. They are mazelike and full of hazards such as quicksand, poisonous snakes, and insects. Since Mary Ann Townsend was probably never able to return for her treasure in the marshes of South Carolina, it may very well still be there.

South Dakota
The Fabulous Stolen Loot from the Unrobbable Treasure Coach

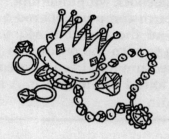

The treasure: About seven hundred pounds of gold dust and gold bars; jewelry and cash

Where it is: A canyon on the northwest side of Table Mountain, near the Badlands National Monument

The Homestake Mining Company of South Dakota was not very worried that their stagecoach shipments of gold might be stolen by bandits. Over the years they had shipped millions of dollars' worth of gold to the U.S. Mint in a fortresslike treasure coach called the *Monitor*. It had never been robbed. The coach was lined with steel, and had no windows except for small gun portholes. Inside it carried a special chest that held the gold. The chest was so difficult to open that the mine owners believed it would take at least a day for any robber to break into it.

But on September 26, 1878, the mining company's treasure proved too hard for one gang to pass up. When the treasure coach stopped to change horses in Canyon Springs, Wyoming, the gang of five robbers began shooting. It took several hours, but the outlaws managed to steal the money, diamonds, jewelry, and an estimated seven hundred pounds of gold. The outlaws fled on horseback with their loot.

The stagecoach company offered a $2,500 reward for the return of the treasure. Many joined in the search, hoping to earn the reward. In just weeks, bits of the stolen treasure had been located and returned. It was not all found in one place. A single gold bar

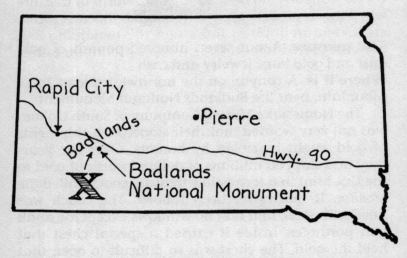

was found near a campfire. One gang member was captured and led authorities to gold dust that he had buried.

Another gold bar was found displayed in a bank window. It quickly led officers to one of the robbers. He turned out to be Thomas Goodale, the bank president's son and the last of the outlaws alive by this time. Goodale confessed that the rest of the treasure was buried at Table Mountain. But he escaped and disappeared before showing anyone the precise location. Finding the treasure seemed hopeless after his disappearance, and interest in the treasure died down.

But in 1933, a rancher found one of the gold bars near Table Mountain, and interest in finding this treasure was renewed. It is estimated that the stagecoach was carrying about $400,000' worth of treasure when it was robbed. Only a fraction of this was recovered. Treasure hunters think that the remaining loot remains buried somewhere on Table Mountain to this day.

Tennessee
The Lost Coin Kegs of Farmer Wenten

The treasure: A large fortune in gold and silver coins
Where it is: Near Hillsboro, along State Highway 41, in Coffee County

During the last years of the Civil War, times were tough in Coffee County. Most people living in the area were poor. There was little law enforcement and bands of outlaws roamed the countryside looting and robbing.

Most people in Coffee County knew that Cephus Wenten (or Cese Wenton) was a successful farmer. They also thought that he was rich and stingy

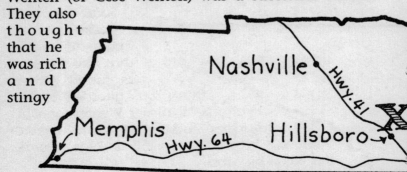

with his money. Wenten did not trust banks and preferred to keep his money hidden. It is believed that he buried over $50,000' worth of gold and silver coins in kegs around his farm.

When a local outlaw gang heard the tales of Wenten's wealth, they headed for his farm. They were determined to steal his money no matter what it took. The desperadoes attacked Wenten and demanded that he tell them the location of his coins. But he refused. Though they beat him and eventually hanged him, Wenten never revealed his treasure's whereabouts. Wenten hadn't told his family the location of the treasure, so they could not tell, either. They were also killed. The gang dug aimlessly around the farm hoping to luck into finding the treasure. But they found nothing and eventually gave up.

About sixty years later, the Wenten farm lay abandoned. While poking through the ruins of the farm, a man discovered one of Wenten's coin-filled kegs. He told a friend about the keg, and the friend went to dig it up. But before he could, he mysteriously died.

Knoxville

Some people in Coffee County began to believe that the treasure was cursed. Others think it is guarded by the ghosts of farmer Wenten and his murdered family. As far as anyone knows, Wenten's coin-filled kegs remain buried on his farm.

Texas
Emperor Maximilian's Treasure

The treasure: Emperor Maximilian's fortune of gold and jewels, worth an estimated $5 million
Where it is: Castle Gap, Texas.

In 1864, France's Emperor, Napoléon III, appointed Austrian Archduke Ferdinand Maximilian as emperor of Mexico. Napoléon hoped this would help France gain more power in North America. However, the United States soon demanded that Napoléon withdraw all troops from Mexico. As Napoléon's troops began to leave in early 1866, supporters of Mexican president Benito Juarez began to reconquer Mexico.

Emperor Maximilian quickly realized that he would be overthrown by the Mexicans once the protection of the French army was gone. During his reign in Mexico he had stolen great riches from the country. He decided to send this treasure back to Austria, where he thought it would be safest. Maximilian packed his riches into barrels for transport. His treasure was so vast that it took forty-five barrels to hold it. Before sealing each barrel, he added a layer of flour on top of the treasure. He hoped this would fool anyone who happened to look inside into thinking the barrels were full of flour. Maximilian told his Austrian officers to take the barrels north to the port of Galveston, Texas. From there they could be shipped to his home in Austria.

In February 1866, Maximilian's officers left Mexico with the treasure barrels loaded on fifteen wagons. One night after they had crossed the Rio Grande River into Texas, six soldiers from the recently defeated Confederate army wandered into their camp. The soldiers warned them that Indians and Mexican bandits were waiting on the road ahead to attack them. The Austrian officers offered one hundred dollars to each of the six soldiers to go with them and help guard their flour shipment. The ex-Confederate soldiers quickly agreed.

But they were suspicious. Why would the Austrians pay them so much to guard barrels of flour? The soldiers secretly peeked inside the barrels one night and discovered they were full of treasure. They plotted to steal it.

Soon after they passed through Castle Gap, Texas, the soldiers killed the Austrians and burned their wagons. They took as much of the treasure as they could carry in their saddlebags and buried the rest, planning to return for it later.

As they made their getaway, one of the soldiers suddenly became sick. The others suspected that he was just faking. They thought he was trying to trick them into leaving him behind so that he could sneak back alone for the treasure. They shot him and

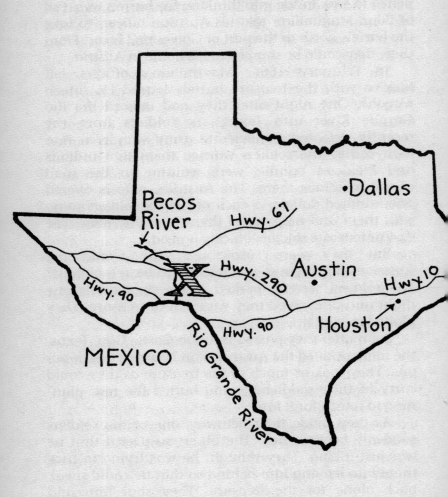

Pecos
River

Hwy. 67

•Dallas

Hwy. 290

Austin
•

Hwy. 10

Hwy. 90

Hwy. 90

Houston

MEXICO

Rio Grande River

continued on their way, leaving him for dead. But the soldier didn't die after all, and somehow managed to follow the others. To his surprise, they were all dead when he caught up with them. They had been killed by Indians.

The wounded soldier was able to reach a nearby town, where a doctor tried to save him. It was hopeless. As he lay dying, he realized that he didn't want the treasure to be lost forever. He told the doctor that a great treasure belonging to Maximilian was buried under the bones of the murdered Austrians and their burned wagons. He drew a map showing its location.

The doctor was unable to look for the treasure immediately after the soldier died, due to hostile Indians in the area. He finally began searching ten years later. Some of the clues to the treasure's location on the soldier's map included the following: There was a big lake near the treasure. There was also a rock with a window in it somewhere nearby. By looking through this window, the spot where the treasure was buried could be seen by someone standing with his or her back to Castle Mountain.

But after ten years, sandstorms had changed or hidden landmarks on the treasure map. The doctor couldn't locate the treasure.

Emperor Maximilian never saw his treasure again, either. He was captured by Mexican fighters and executed on June 19, 1867. The location of his famous treasure is believed to be about fifteen miles east of Horsehead Crossing on the Pecos River, between Highways 67 and 90.

Utah
Lost Mormon Gold

The treasure: Over 200 ten-dollar Mormon gold coins, possibly worth as much as $75,000 each today

Where it is: South of the Great Salt Lake, in the Sevier Desert

In 1847, Brigham Young and a group of Mormons left Illinois and moved west to seek religious freedom. They settled near the Great Salt Lake in Utah and founded Salt Lake City. Over the next few years, many settlers and prospectors passed through Salt Lake City on their way to California and Nevada. They often stopped to buy supplies from the Mormons before continuing westward across the desert.

Before the 1849 California gold rush, purchases were made using the barter or trading system. But after 1849, many travelers began to insist on using gold or money. This presented a problem. The Mormons needed gold to run their businesses. It is believed that Ute Indians helped out by showing Brigham Young a rich gold mine known only to their tribe. The Indians made Young promise to keep the mine's location a secret.

Thanks to the Utes, Young now had gold. But he still needed to turn it into coins that could be spent easily. The United States government had a mint in Philadelphia, and many gold mines sent their raw gold there to be made into coins. But this took a long time. Young's solution was to open a private mint so the Mormons could quickly make their own gold coins. Using the gold from the Indians' mine, the Mormons produced $2.50, $5, $10, and $20 gold coins. On one side of each coin was a beehive. Joined hands were stamped on the reverse side.

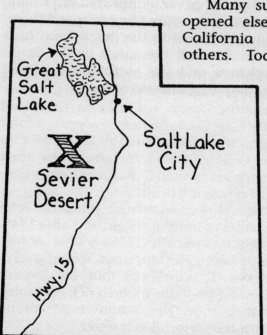

Many such mints were opened elsewhere in both California and Utah by others. Today, only the federal government can create money in the United States, so all of these private mints are now closed.

The Mormons proudly showed off their mint and gave tours to

visitors. Two greedy brothers named Dave and Reg Baldwin took a tour of the mint one day and noticed that it was unguarded. The brothers returned several nights later and stole about 200 ten-dollar gold coins. They hoped no one would notice if they were careful not to take too much. Their plot worked. For several days, the Mormons didn't realize they had been robbed. Once the money was missed, the Mormons tracked the Baldwin brothers into the desert south of the Great Salt Lake. But their trail soon disappeared. Neither the brothers nor the coins were ever found.

Since the gold pieces never reappeared anywhere, it is clear that the Baldwins didn't live to spend them. The brothers may have died in the desert from heat and lack of water. Beneath the sands of the Sevier Desert, their skeletons and the Mormon's lost gold coins may lie waiting to be discovered.

Vermont
Bristol Treasure Chests

The treasure: Four treasure chests filled with millions of dollars' worth of gold coins

Where it is: In a cave at the base of South Mountain, southeast of Bristol, Vermont

The trading ship *Nebuchadnezzar* sailed along the Atlantic Coast from South Carolina to Nova Scotia, Canada, in the 1760s. Its captain was hard on his crew, and they did not like him. He was known as "Bloody Charles." The crew watched over the years as the captain slowly filled eight wooden sea chests with gold coins he earned on their many trading voyages. And they grew jealous.

One night in 1765, the *Nebuchadnezzar* docked at Boston, Massachusetts. The captain went into town to enjoy the evening. But he made the crew remain behind on the ship under guard. He would not allow them to go into town and have fun. A crew member named Phillip DeGrau suggested to the rest of the sailors that they steal the captain's gold while he was gone. They were all angry at the captain and quickly

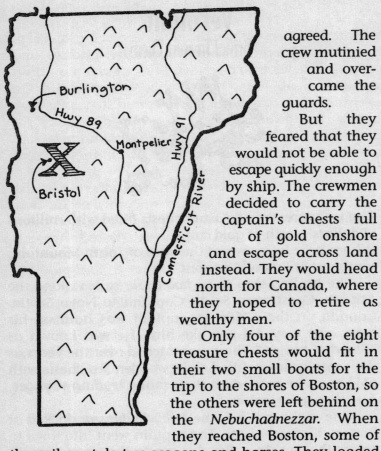

agreed. The crew mutinied and overcame the guards.

But they feared that they would not be able to escape quickly enough by ship. The crewmen decided to carry the captain's chests full of gold onshore and escape across land instead. They would head north for Canada, where they hoped to retire as wealthy men.

Only four of the eight treasure chests would fit in their two small boats for the trip to the shores of Boston, so the others were left behind on the *Nebuchadnezzar*. When they reached Boston, some of the sailors stole two wagons and horses. They loaded two chests on each wagon and headed for Canada.

One of the wagons broke down in the Green Mountains of Vermont, so the sailors loaded all four chests onto the one remaining wagon. Travel was almost impossible with such a heavy load on just one wagon. The men voted to bury the chests for safekeeping and go in search of new wagons, fresh horses, and supplies. They found a cave at the foot of a mountain and buried all four chests there. The men hid the opening to the cave with branches and stones. As they traveled on toward Canada, they hoped to return for the treasure one day. No one knows what happened to the sailors, but they didn't return as planned. Except for one.

In 1790, DeGrau did return to search in vain for the cave. The people in the nearby town of Pocock grew curious about what he was doing, and he told them about the treasure. This is how this treasure legend began. DeGrau never found the cave or his treasure, and he returned to Canada without it. One possible reason that he could not find his cave again was that a 1776 earthquake had caused rock slides in the Green Mountains. The landscape had changed, so landmarks pointing to the cave might have disappeared.

The town of Pocock is now known as Bristol. The area where DeGrau's treasure is believed to be buried is known as the Bristol Money Diggings. People still search for it.

Virginia
Thomas Beale's Secret Treasure Codes

The treasure: Gold, silver, and jewels worth between $20 and $35 million

Where it is: The Blue Ridge Mountains of Virginia

In 1822, Thomas Beale visited his friend Robert Morriss and gave him a mysterious box. Beale told him to open the locked iron box if he did not come back within ten years. Beale left and never returned.

Morriss finally broke the lock and opened the box after waiting over twenty years. Inside he found three secret codes! There were also letters from Beale, which told a fantastic tale. He wrote that he and some other men had discovered silver and gold in mines 250 miles north of Santa Fe, New Mexico. They had mined for a year and a half and had hidden most of their treasure in a secret location.

Beale's letters said that his first code told where the treasure was located. The second code listed the contents of the treasure. The third code was a list of the people who should get a share, including Morriss. Beale wrote that he would send the keys to decipher

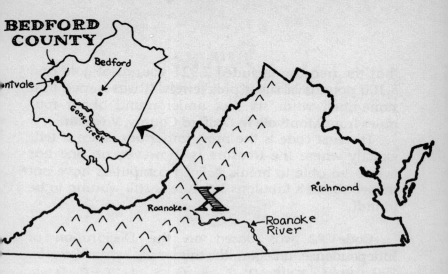

BEDFORD COUNTY

Bedford

ntvale

Goose Creek

Richmond

Roanoke

Roanoke River

the codes, but he never did. No one knows what happened to him.

Morriss couldn't figure out the codes on his own. Shortly before he died in 1863, he showed them to his friend James Ward. Ward broke the second code many years later by comparing it to the Declaration of Independence.

Here's how the second code works: Number each word in the Declaration, from 1 to 1322. The first number in Beale's code is 115. The 115th word in the Declaration is "instituted," which begins with the letter "I." So the first letter in Beale's code is "I." Only the first letter of each word in the Declaration is used.

The Declaration of Independence was written by Thomas Jefferson. Beale's full name was Thomas Jefferson Beale. Maybe that's what gave him the idea for the second code!

Once the second code was deciphered, it explained

that the treasure included 2,921 pounds of gold and 5,100 pounds of silver plus jewels. It was buried in a stone-lined vault six feet underground about four miles from Montvale in Bedford County, Virginia.

The first code is the most important, since it tells exactly where the treasure is. However, no one has ever been able to break it. Even computers have not helped. Beale's fabulous treasure is still waiting to be found!

Code #2 was based on the Declaration of Independence. It began like this:

I	H	A	V	E	D	E	P	O	S	I	T	E	D
115	73	24	818	37	52	49	17	31	62	657	22	7	15

The 115th word in the Declaration is "instituted." Just use the first letter of this word. So the first word in Beale's code #2 was "I." The 73rd word in the Declaration is "hold." Just use this word's first letter. So the second letter in Beale's code was "h." And so on.

. . . That to secure these rights, governments are **instituted** among men, deriving their just powers . . .
115

73
. . . We **hold** these truths to be self-evident, that all men are created equal, that they are endowed by their Creator with certain unalienable rights, that among these are life, liberty, and the pursuit of happiness . . .

Code #1 has never been broken. It is the most important code because it tells where the treasure is. Code #1 is shown below. Can you figure it out?

71, 194, 38, 1701, 89, 76, 11, 83, 1629, 48, 94, 63, 132, 16, 111, 95, 84, 341, 975, 14, 40, 64, 27, 81, 139, 213, 63, 90, 1120, 8, 15, 3, 126, 2018, 40, 74, 758, 485, 604, 230, 436, 664, 582, 150, 251, 284, 308, 231, 124, 211, 486, 225, 401, 370, 11, 101, 305, 139, 189, 17, 33, 88, 208, 193, 145, 1, 94, 73, 416, 918, 263, 28, 500, 538, 356, 117, 136, 219, 27, 176, 130, 10, 460, 25, 485, 18, 436, 65, 84, 200, 283, 118, 320, 138, 36, 416, 280, 15, 71, 224, 961, 44, 16, 401, 39, 88, 61, 304, 12, 21, 24, 283, 134, 92, 63, 246, 486, 682, 7, 219, 184, 360, 780, 18, 64, 463, 474, 131, 160, 79, 73, 440, 95, 18, 64, 581, 34, 69, 128, 367, 460, 17, 81, 12, 103, 820, 62, 110, 97, 103, 862, 70, 60, 1317, 471, 540, 208, 121, 890, 346, 36, 150, 59, 568, 614, 13, 120, 63, 219, 812, 2160, 1780, 99, 35, 18, 21, 136, 872, 15, 28, 170, 88, 4, 30, 44, 112, 18, 147, 436, 195, 320, 37, 122, 113, 6, 140, 8, 120, 305, 42, 58, 461, 44, 106, 301, 13, 408, 680, 93, 86, 116, 530, 82, 568, 9, 102, 38, 416, 89, 71, 216, 728, 965, 818, 2, 38, 121, 195, 14, 326, 148, 234, 18, 55, 131, 234, 361, 824, 5, 81, 623, 48, 961, 19, 26, 33, 10, 1101, 365, 92, 88, 181, 275, 346, 201, 206, 86, 36, 219, 324, 829, 840, 64, 326, 19, 48, 122, 85, 216, 284, 919, 861, 326, 985, 233, 64, 68, 232, 431, 960, 50, 29, 81, 216, 321, 603, 14, 612, 81, 360, 36, 51, 62, 194, 78, 60, 200, 314, 676, 112, 4, 28, 18, 61, 136, 247, 819, 921, 1060, 464, 895, 10, 6, 66, 119, 38, 41, 49, 602, 423, 962, 302, 294, 875, 78, 14, 23, 111, 109, 62, 31, 501, 823, 216, 280, 34, 24, 150, 1000, 162, 286, 19, 21, 17, 340, 19, 242, 31, 86, 234, 140, 607, 115, 33, 191, 67, 104, 86, 52, 88, 16, 80, 121, 67, 95, 122, 216, 548, 96, 11, 201, 77, 364, 218, 65, 667, 890, 236, 154, 211, 10, 98, 34, 119, 56, 216, 119, 71, 218, 1164, 1496, 1817, 51, 39, 210, 36, 3, 19, 540, 232, 22, 141, 617, 84, 290, 80, 46, 207, 411, 150, 29, 38, 46, 172, 85, 194, 39, 261, 543, 897, 624, 18, 212, 416, 127, 931, 19, 4, 63, 96, 12, 101, 418, 16, 140, 230, 460, 538, 19, 27, 88, 612, 1431, 90, 716, 275, 74, 83, 11, 426, 89, 72, 84, 1300, 1706, 814, 221, 132, 40, 102, 34, 868, 975, 1101, 84, 16, 79, 23, 16, 81, 122, 324, 403, 912, 227, 936, 447, 55, 86, 34, 43, 212, 107, 96, 314, 264, 1065, 323, 428, 601, 203, 124, 95, 216, 814, 2906, 654, 820, 2, 301, 112, 176, 213, 71, 87, 96, 202, 35, 10, 2, 41, 17, 84, 221, 736, 820, 214, 11, 60, 760.

Washington
D. B. Cooper's Thanksgiving Treasure

The treasure: Nearly $200,000 in twenty-dollar bills
Where it is: Somewhere in southwestern Washington

On the night before Thanksgiving in 1971, Dan (D. B.) Cooper pulled a surprising caper that probably either killed him or made him rich. He set his plan in motion when he boarded an airplane in Portland, Oregon. The plane took off, heading north toward Seattle, Washington. During the flight, Cooper told a flight attendant that he was carrying a dynamite bomb. He demanded a parachute and $200,000 in twenty-dollar bills. Cooper threatened to blow up the plane if he didn't get them. His request was radioed ahead to Seattle police.

When the plane arrived in Seattle, the $200,000 and the parachute were delivered to Cooper. He let all of the passengers leave the plane. Then he and the crew took off again, flying toward Nevada. The plane was somewhere over southwest Washington when Cooper parachuted out with the stolen money. D. B. Cooper was never seen or heard from again.

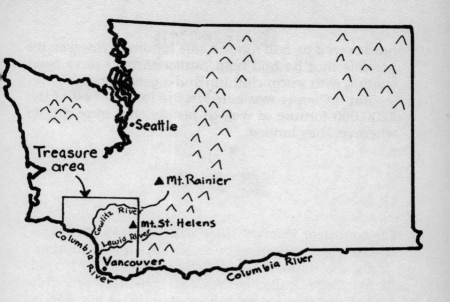

The FBI later determined that Cooper must have bailed out somewhere within a twenty-five-square-mile area. But no one knew exactly where. One clue came when an eight-year-old boy found $5,880 along the Columbia River a few miles northwest of Vancouver, Washington. The serial numbers of the money given to Cooper had been recorded by the FBI, so it was easy to tell that the boy's money was part of Cooper's loot.

But what had happened to Cooper and the rest of the money? Had he landed safely? The crew of the plane he hijacked said he did not seem to be an experienced sky diver. It was cold and stormy on the November night that Cooper jumped, and he was not warmly dressed. Escaping on foot would have been hard even if he had made a safe landing. However, it's possible that he had help. Someone may have been waiting with warm clothing and a getaway car.

But if Cooper was killed in the fall, the rest of the $200,000 fortune as well as his skeleton may still lie wherever they landed.

West Virginia
Dollhouse Dollars

The treasure: $330,000
Where it is: Upshur County, in the Appalachian Mountains of West Virginia

In 1889, there was a bank robbery just east of Upshur County, in the Appalachian Mountains. About $330,000 was stolen, but the robber was never caught. A few weeks after the robbery, a stranger named Alfonso Marzo arrived in an Appalachian Mountain valley. He carried all of his belongings in one small trunk and a large sack.

Marzo soon built and settled into a tiny cabin. His neighbors nicknamed it the "dollhouse" because it looked like a child's dollhouse. Marzo was a loner and didn't have many friends. His neighbors noticed that though he didn't seem to have a job, he still had plenty of money. In 1894, Marzo suddenly disappeared from the valley.

Around 1911, one of Marzo's neighbors received a mysterious letter from him. Marzo wrote that he was in a prison in Madrid, Spain! He claimed that he had

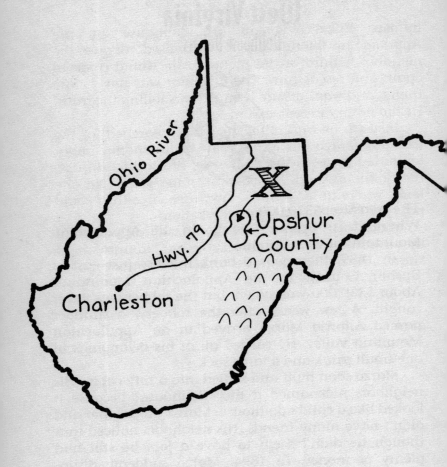

Ohio River

X

Hwy. 79

Upshur
County

Charleston

hidden $330,000 near his dollhouse in the Appalachian Mountains. He promised to give the neighbor a third of the money if he would come to Spain and rescue him. The neighbor was not a close friend, and was not sure if Marzo was telling the truth. He did not try to rescue Marzo.

Instead, he and other neighbors searched for the treasure. Marzo's neighbor thought the money might be buried beneath the dollhouse. But to his surprise, the dollhouse had vanished over the years. No one knew where to look for the treasure, since they could not recall the house's original location.

Today, it is believed that the house was located in the southeastern section of Upshur County, near Shahan Farm. No one has ever found this treasure.

Wisconsin
John Dillinger's Bank Loot

The treasure: $100,000 or more of stolen money
Where it is: About five hundred yards north of the Little Bohemia Lodge, near Rhinelander, Wisconsin, off U.S. Highway 51

During the Great Depression of the 1930s, an outlaw named John Dillinger robbed dozens of banks in the Midwestern United States. Other bank robbers of the time, such as Bonnie and Clyde, usually stole small amounts of money. But Dillinger often made off with huge sums in his robberies. He became so notorious that he was declared among the first "Public Enemies" in history by the FBI.

Dillinger was captured in January 1934, in Arizona. He was sent to Indiana to go on trial for murder. However, he made a famous escape from the high-security jail in Crown Point, Indiana. He fooled the guards with a fake pistol carved from a bar of soap (or from wood) and blackened to look realistic. Within days of his escape he had stolen another $100,000 from banks in South Dakota and Iowa.

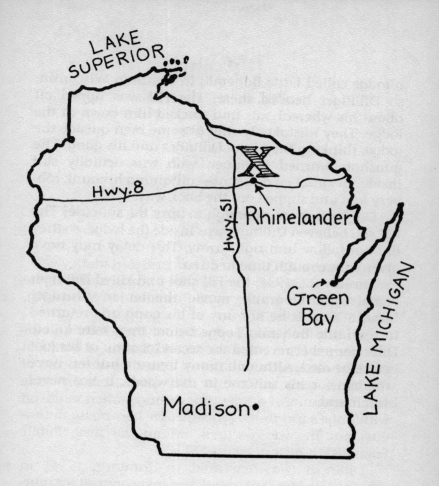

During the Iowa robbery all did not go as planned, and Dillinger was wounded. He went to Saint Paul, Minnesota for medical treatment. Someone recognized him and alerted FBI agents, who quickly moved in to arrest him in April 1934.

Dillinger needed a place to hide. A friend suggested

a lodge called Little Bohemia in northern Wisconsin, so Dillinger headed there. The FBI was tipped off about his whereabouts and tracked him down at the lodge. They mistakenly shot at some men outside the lodge, thinking they were Dillinger and his gang. The gunshots warned Dillinger, who was actually still inside. He grabbed a suitcase containing his bank robbery loot and slipped out the back way.

Did he stop long enough to bury the suitcase? The FBI still believed Dillinger was inside the lodge, so they did not follow him right away. This delay may have given him enough time to do so.

On July 22, 1934, the FBI shot and killed Dillinger outside the Biograph movie theater in Chicago, Illinois. Neither he nor any of his gang had returned to the Little Bohemia Lodge before they were killed. Dillinger never revealed the secret location of his loot before he died. Although many treasure hunters have searched for his suitcase in the woods, it has never been found.

Wyoming
Cattle Kate's Buried Treasure

The treasure: $50,000 or more worth of gold and silver coins

Where it is: The Sweetwater River Valley, in southwest Wyoming

Cattle Kate's real name was Ella Watson. She was a large, beautiful woman who rode a horse well and was handy with a gun. Watson arrived in Wyoming when she was twenty-six. She was soon rustling cattle in cahoots with a man named Jim Averill.

Averill owned a ranch and saloon, and rustled cattle from large ranches in the Sweetwater River Valley area. Small ranchers like Jim Averill were not friendly with the large cattle ranchers in the valley. Small ranchers thought that the large ranchers were running them out of business. To fight back, some of them rustled the large ranchers' cattle, put their own brand on them, and resold them.

Ella Watson built a cabin with a corral about a mile away from Averill's saloon. Stolen cattle were kept there until they could be driven to Cheyenne,

Wyoming, to be sent by train for sale elsewhere.

Averill and Watson lived the good life as a result of their crimes. Jim Averill was seen smoking cigars and wearing a gold watch on his vest. Ella Watson exchanged her old buckskin dress for new flowered gowns and spiffy button-up shoes.

But their prosperity came to an end one day in 1889, when some cattlemen from the larger ranches got angry. They wanted to put a stop to the rustling of their cattle. Legend has it that these ranchers kidnapped Watson and Averill and took them to the

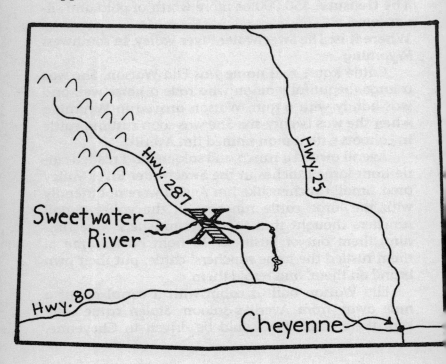

Sweetwater River. They tied ropes around the two rustlers' necks and warned that they would hang them unless they promised to stop stealing cattle.

Watson was afraid. She told the cattlemen that she had saved more than $50,000 in gold and silver coins, which she had buried near her cabin. She wanted to tell them where the money was buried, in hopes that they would then let her go. But Averill thought the cattlemen were bluffing, and told her to keep quiet. Watson and Averill both refused to agree to stop rustling. They were soon hanged from a cottonwood tree on the banks of the river. The cattlemen returned to Watson's cabin and rounded up their stolen cattle. They searched for Watson's buried coins, but were unable to find them.

In 1929, a letter believed to have been written by Ella Watson was found in an old trunk. It was a letter to her family, telling them about the fortune she had made rustling cattle. She wrote that she had buried her coins about six feet deep in a well near her cabin. Though treasure hunters have searched, Ella Watson's fortune has never been found.

Alberta, Canada
The Lost Lemon Mine

The treasure: An incredibly rich gold mine
Where it is: In the Highland Mountains, near the Highwood River

In 1870, two men named "Blackjack" and "Lemon" and some other prospectors from Montana headed to the North Saskatchewan River, in Canada, to search for gold. Along the Elk River, Blackjack and Lemon split off from the rest of the group and followed an old Indian trail. They noticed bits of gold in a mountain stream and followed the stream hoping to find its source. They struck pay dirt—a rich vein of gold!

That night as they camped, the two men began to argue. They couldn't agree on whether to stay through the upcoming winter or leave and return in the spring to mine the gold. After Blackjack fell asleep, Lemon quietly crawled over to him and killed him with an ax. Lemon regretted it almost immediately. He returned to Montana and confessed to a priest what he had done. A man was sent to bury

Blackjack's body, and he marked the grave. But as soon as he finished the burial and left, Indians destroyed the grave marker. Two young Stoney Indians had secretly watched Blackjack and Lemon discover the gold and had seen Lemon kill Blackjack. The Indians thought prospectors were trouble, and did not want more to come.

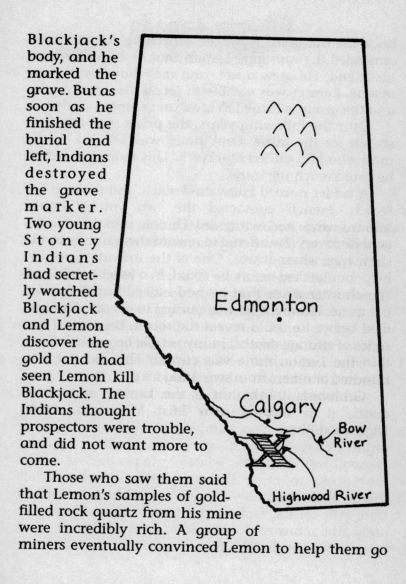

Those who saw them said that Lemon's samples of gold-filled rock quartz from his mine were incredibly rich. A group of miners eventually convinced Lemon to help them go back for the gold. However, searching for the mine reminded the unhappy Lemon that he had murdered his friend. He grew upset, and may have even gone insane. Lemon was unable to locate the gold again, and the group returned to Montana empty-handed.

Over the following years, the priest sent others to search for the mine. One group was headed by the man who had buried Blackjack. This man died before he could reach the mine.

A trader named Lafayette French also took up the search. French contacted the two young Stoney Indians who had witnessed Lemon and Blackjack's gold discovery. He offered to reward them if they would show him where it was. One of the Indians agreed to help, but he died before he could. In a letter to a friend, French later wrote that he had indeed finally located the mine. However, he was burned in an accident and died before he could reveal the secret. Because of this series of strange deaths, many people began to believe that the Lemon mine was cursed. This did not stop hundred of others from searching for it.

Geologists think that if the Lemon mine truly exists, it is located near Mist Mountain, along Highwood River.

British Columbia, Canada
Ghost Town Treasure

The treasure: $20,000 in gold bars
Where it is: McMynn's Meadows, near the ghost town of Camp McKinney, British Columbia

Camp McKinney is a lonely ghost town today. But in the 1890s it was a thriving community located near the Cariboo Gold Mine. It was also the scene of a gold shipment robbery.

One day in August 1896, a man whose last name was Roderick hatched a sneaky plan. He did not go to his job at the mine that day. Instead, he took some whiskey and hid along a wagon trail. He was waiting for a wagon scheduled to leave the mine camp with a shipment of gold bars. As usual, only the wagon driver accompanied the gold. No guards were used because the wagon's route was so treacherous that no one thought a bandit would dare attempt a robbery. Less than an hour outside of the camp, Roderick held up the gold wagon at gunpoint.

When the wagon driver later reported the robbery back in camp, a search party was sent out. The only

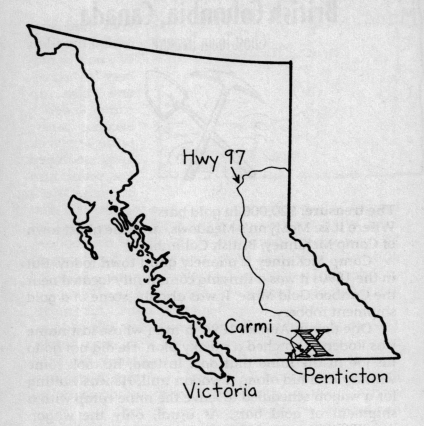

Hwy 97

Carmi

Penticton

Victoria

clues Roderick had left behind were an empty whiskey bottle and empty saddlebags. The gold was nowhere to be found. In fact, no one even realized that Roderick had been the robber.

Recovering the missing gold seemed impossible—until authorities got a tip. Just a few days before, Rod-

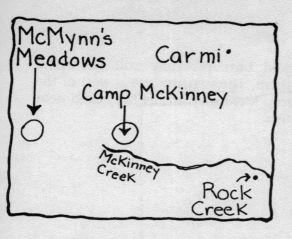

erick had suggested the idea of such a robbery to someone else in camp! Roderick became their prime suspect. They searched and found him in Seattle, Washington. However, he was not living the life of a rich man. What had become of the gold? Lawmen decided he must have hidden it near the site of the robbery, and then left Camp McKinney to wait for things to cool down. They staked out the place where Roderick was living and secretly watched him.

A few weeks later, Roderick made his move. The police stayed carefully hidden as they followed him from Seattle northward across the Canadian border. Soon Roderick was back in Camp McKinney, believing that no one realized he was the gold thief. A few days after his return, he rode out of camp on horseback. He headed west with the police hot on his trail.

Sometime later, Roderick stopped near McMynn's Meadows to rest his horse. Thinking he had stopped to dig up the gold, the police accidentally shot him. They were upset when they realized their mistake. The gold was nowhere nearby, and now Roderick was dead. They had ruined any chance to ask him where the gold was hidden.

The stolen gold bars probably still lie where Roderick buried them. The treasure site is west of the ghost town of Camp McKinney, in the hilly area near McMynn's Meadows.

Nova Scotia, Canada
The Oak Island Money Pit

The treasure: Pirate gold and jewels?
Where it is: Oak Island, in Nova Scotia, Canada

In 1795, three boys found clues on Oak Island that made them think a treasure had been buried there. The first clue was a round, sunken place in the ground. It was thirteen feet across. The second clue was an oak tree limb hanging above the circle. The limb had been cut short, and an old ship's block and tackle hung from it.

The three boys knew pirates had visited Oak Island many times. Had a rope been used on this block and tackle to lower pirate treasure from the limb deep into the ground below? The boys thought so. They got shovels from home and dug down as far as thirty feet. They found a stone slab and some wooden log platforms. But they never found a treasure.

When one of the boys grew up, he went back to Oak Island in 1804 to try again. He and his team dug deeper still. Every ten feet down, they found another wood platform. Some were covered with

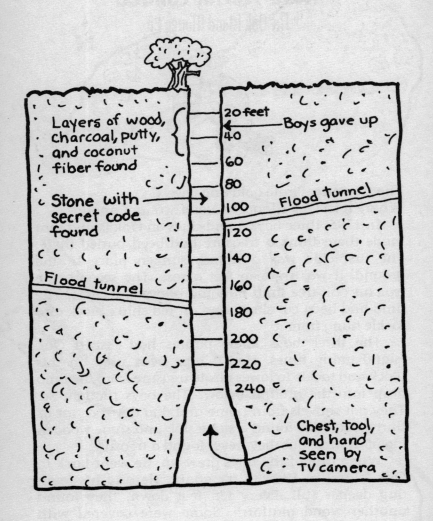

Layers of wood, charcoal, putty, and coconut fiber found

20 feet

Boys gave up

40

60

80

Stone with secret code found

100

Flood tunnel

120

140

Flood tunnel

160

180

200

220

240

Chest, tool, and hand seen by TV camera

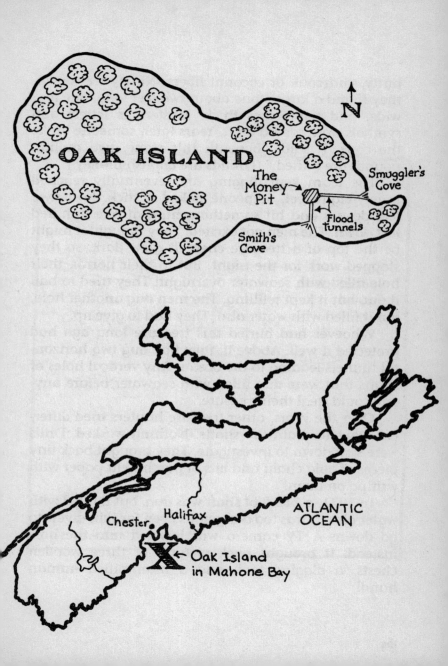

putty, charcoal, or coconut fibers. Ninety feet down, they found a large stone about two feet long, one foot wide, and ten inches thick. Mysterious letters and symbols were carved on it. Years later, someone broke the code. It said: "Beneath this stone, two million pounds are buried." (Pounds are English money.)

The team kept digging and eventually reached ninety-eight feet. Someone poked a stick down two feet deeper and hit something hard at one hundred feet down. The men got excited. They thought it might be the top of a treasure chest. It grew dark, so they stopped work for the night. But to their horror, their hole filled with seawater overnight! They tried to bail it out, but it kept refilling. The men dug another hole, but it filled with water also. They had to give up.

Whoever had buried this treasure long ago had protected it well. Above it, they had dug two horizontal tunnels leading to the ocean. Any vertical holes or shafts that were dug filled with seawater before anyone could steal their treasure.

Over the years, other treasure hunters tried different ways to drain the shafts. Nothing worked. Drills were sent down to investigate. They brought back tiny pieces of gold chain and bits of parchment paper with writing on them!

In 1971, a 212-foot shaft was dug, but it filled with water also. It was too dangerous even for skin divers to go down. A TV camera was lowered into the hole instead. It brought back pictures of three wooden chests, a digging tool, and a mummified human hand!

Whose treasure is buried on Oak Island? Some people think it belonged to pirates. But others think it could be Marie Antoinette's jewels, British Army, treasure, or Inca gold.

The location of this treasure has been known for two hundred years. Many have tried, but no one has been able to get it as yet. Even Franklin D. Roosevelt invested money trying to find this treasure, before he became a U.S. president. Treasure hunters have cut down many of the oak trees and dug many holes on the island in their searches.

How do you think the people who hid this treasure planned to get it back out again themselves? Is there another entrance? If you can figure this out, maybe you'll help uncover this treasure at last!

Quebec, Canada
Lost French Treasure

The treasure: Gold, doubloons and jewels, worth an estimated $2,500,000

Where it is: The Saint Charles River, near Quebec

In 1791, Quebec became part of Canada. But in 1747, it was under French rule and was the center of an area called New France. The fortress in Quebec protected a large treasure belonging to the colonists of New France. These colonists lived in the Quebec area and believed that their money would be safest in the fort.

The British had made many attempts to capture Quebec over the years. When British General James Wolfe attacked Quebec in September 1759, the leader of the French army, the Marquis de Montcalm, decided that this treasure had to be moved. He thought that the treasure belonging to Quebec's more than seven thousand colonists might be safer hidden elsewhere for a while.

The treasure was placed in chests and sacks, and was buried along the nearby Saint Charles River. The

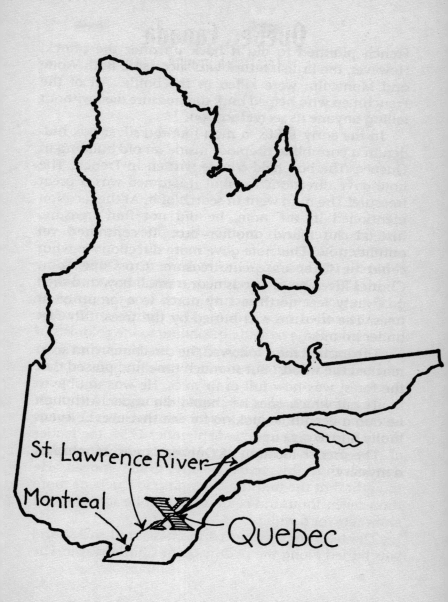

St. Lawrence River

Montreal

Quebec

French planned to dig it back up after the attack. However, the British attack was successful. Both Wolfe and Montcalm were killed in the battle. All of the Frenchmen who helped bury the treasure died without telling anyone its secret location.

In the early 1900s, a man found a silver box hidden in a crumbling fireplace inside an old building in Quebec. The box held a note written in French. The note gave directions to what it claimed was a great treasure! The man went in search of it. At the location mentioned in the note, he did not find treasure. Instead, he found another box. It contained yet another note. This note gave more directions to what could be Quebec's great treasure: Cross the Saint Charles River, go to woods near a small bay, and then go twenty feet northwest by north to a group of fir trees. The treasure was buried by the trees, fifty feet underground.

The excited man followed the directions, and soon reached the woods. But so much time had passed that the forest was now full of fir trees. He was unable to figure out which ones he should dig under. Although he dug a deep hole looking for the treasure, he eventually had to give up.

The precise location of Quebec's treasure remains a mystery.

Some Helpful Hints
Finders-keepers?

Who owns found treasure? Does it belong to the people who lost it and their families? Or does it belong to whomever finds it?

If you find a treasure on someone else's property, the treasure does not belong to you. Never trespass. Always get the owner's permission before hunting on private property. Some treasure hunters are able to write an agreement with landowners to share any treasure they might find.

If you find stolen, lost, or hidden treasure, it must be returned to its original owner. There is often a waiting period to see if a treasure is claimed. If an owner can't be found, or if no one can prove they own it, you may get to keep it!

Sunken treasure found far out in the ocean may belong to the finder. But it might also belong to the owners of nearby land or to nearby countries.

If you discover a historical treasure, such as Hawaiian King Kamehameha's, do not touch it. Archaeologists will want to study it just the way you first found it.

Cities, counties, states, and countries all have laws governing treasure hunting and ownership of found treasure. It's very important that each treasure hunter learn and obey these laws. Lost treasure locations are often hazardous. Treasure hunters should take necessary safety measures and be cautious.

Where can treasure clues be found?
You may be lucky and find a treasure by guessing. But true treasure hunters look for clues before they begin a search.

Good places to look for treasure clues are in old newspapers or books in the library. The library lists books about treasure under the topics of "treasure hunting" or "treasure trove." Old books, maps, diaries, journals, and photos in library history collections may also hold clues.

Treasure magazines can yield clues too. Your local library may carry them, or you can subscribe yourself. Some well-known magazines about treasures and treasure-hunting are: *Lost Treasure*; *Treasure*; *Treasure Quest*; *and Western & Eastern Treasures*.

Court records such as land deeds are good clue sources. Look for people who were alive or remember when the treasure was lost. Ask them questions about it.

Checking the Internet may be helpful. Try a search for the name of a particular treasure itself, or search under the names of people and locations associated with the treasure.

Treasure Hunting Websites
These websites may be helpful:

http://www.onlinether.com/resource.htm
A listing of websites about treasure hunting.

http://www.losttreasure.com/treasurebuddies/
Treasure tales, plus information about treasure clubs and associations

To find out more about treasure hunting on the World Wide Web, you can do a search for the words "treasure hunting" or "treasure trove" or "lost treasure" on http://www.yahoo.com or http://www.altavista.com

Pirate Websites

http://www.ecst.csuchico.edu/~beej/pirates/
Photos of pirates, battles, ships, and old pirate maps; links to other pirate websites.

http://ocracoke-nc.com/blackbeard/
Lots of information about the infamous pirate, Blackbeard.

http://dir.yahoo.com/Arts/Humanities/History/
By_Subject/Maritime_History/Piracy/Pirates_and_
Buccaneers/
Yahoo's link to pirate webpages.

To find out more about pirates on the world wide web, you can do a search for the word "pirates" on http://www.yahoo.com or http://www.altavista.com

What equipment does a treasure hunter need?

Your eyes and brain are the most important tools you'll need for treasure hunting. But other tools may be useful as well.

Simple treasure hunting gear includes a shovel and a pick. Always be careful and be sure to get permission from property owners before trespassing or digging. Remember to refill any holes you dig.

Some treasure hunters also use a metal detector. This is a handheld electronic tool that is swung back and forth over the ground. It beeps when it finds metal. But that doesn't always mean you've found treasure. It could just mean you've found an old nail.

A water scoop helps beachcombers search for treasure in shallow water.

A wide, shallow pan can be used to look for gold in a stream. That's where the term "panning for gold" comes from.

Professional treasure hunters may use heavy equipment such as drills, power shovels, cranes, or clamshell scoops.

Sunken treasure is harder and more dangerous to find than treasure on land. Diving gear, a boat, and other costly equipment is needed for the search.

Will you find a lost treasure?

Some people aren't even looking when they find treasure. Some people look for treasure their whole lives and never find any.

There are many lost treasures around the world worth millions of dollars.

Selected References

Book references

The Editors of American Heritage. *Pirates of the Spanish Main*. New York, New York: American Heritage Publishing Co., Inc., 1961.

Andrews, Ernest M. *Georgia's Fabulous Treasure Hoards*. Hapeville, Georgia: Ernest M. Andrews, 1966.

Billett, Michael. *Highwaymen and Outlaws*. New York, New York: Arms and Armour Press, An Imprint of the Cassell Group, Sterling Publishing Co., 1997.

Coates, Robert M. *The Outlaw Years*. New York, New York: The Macaulay Company, 1930.

Coffman, F .L. *1001 Lost, Buried or Sunken Treasures*. New York, New York: Thomas Nelson & Sons.

Conrotto, Eugene L. *Lost Desert Bonanzas*. Palm Desert, California: Desert Southwest Publishers, 1963.

Deem, James M. *How to Hunt Buried Treasure*. New York, New York: Avon Books, 1992, 1994.

Driscoll, Charles B. *Doubloons. The United States of America*. Charles B. Driscoll, 1930.

Groushko, Mike. *Treasure Lost, Found, & Undiscovered.* Philadelphia, Pennsylvania: Courage Books/Running Press, 1990.

Hamilton, Sue L. *"Ma" Barker.* Minneapolis, Minnesota: Abdo & Daughters, 1989.

Haydock, Tim. *Treasure Trove.* New York, New York: Henry Holt and Company, 1986.

Hendricks, George D. *The Bad Man of the West.* San Antonio, Texas: The Naylor Company, 1942 and 1950.

Henson, Michael Paul. *Lost, Buried and Sunken Treasures of the Mid-West.* Jeffersonville, Indiana: Michael Paul Henson, 1973.

Horan, James D. *Desperate Women.* New York, New York: G. P. Putnam's Sons, 1952.

Horan, James D. *The Gunfighters.* New York, Avenel: Gramercy Books, 1976.

Horan, James D. and Sann, Paul. *Pictorial History of the Wild West.* New York, New York: Crown Publishers, Inc., 1954.

Hult, Ruby El. *Lost Mines and Treasures of the Pacific Northwest.* Portland, Oregon: Binfords & Mort, 1957.

Jameson, W. C. *Buried Treasures of the American Southwest.* Little Rock, Arkansas: August House Publishers, Inc., 1989.

Jameson, W. C. *Buried Treasures of the Atlantic Coast.* Little Rock, Arkansas: August House Publishers, Inc., 1998.

Jameson, W. C. *Buried Treasures of the Appalachians.* Little Rock, Arkansas: August House Publishers, Inc.,1991.

Jameson, W. C. *Buried Treasuries of the Great Plains.* Little Rock, Arkansas: August House Publishers, Inc., 1998.

Jameson, W. C. *Buried Treasures of New England.* Little Rock, Arkansas: August House Publihers, Inc., 1998.

Jameson, W. C. *Buried Treasures of the Ozarks.* Little Rock, Arkansas: August House Publishers, Inc., 1990.

Jameson, W. C. *Buried Treasures of the Pacific Northwest.* Little Rock, Arkansas: August House Publishers, Inc., 1995.

Jameson, W. C. *Buried Treasures of the Rocky Mountain West.* Little Rock, Arkansas: August House Publishers, Inc., 1993.

Jameson, W. C. *Buried Treasures of the South.* Little Rock, Arkansas: August House Publishers, Inc., 1992.

Laird, Charlton Grant. *Iowa Legends of Buried Treasure.* Lincoln, Nebraska: Foundation Books, 1990.

Lazeo, Lawrence A. *British Columbia's Treasure World.* New Westminster, British Columbia: L. Lazeo, 1970.

Lincoln, Margarette. *The Pirate's Handbook.* New York, New York: Puffin Books, The Penguin Group, 1995.

Madison, Arnold. *Lost Treasures of America.* Chicago, Illinois; New York, New York; San Francisco, California: Rand McNally & Company, 1977.

Marx, Robert. *Buried Treasures You Can Find.* Dallas, Texas: Ram Publishing Company, 1993.

Marx, Robert F. *Shipwrecks in Florida Waters: A Billion Dollar Graveyard.* Chuluota, Florida: The Mickler House, Publishers, 1979, 1985.

McDonald, Douglas. *Nevada Lost Mines & Buried Treasures.* Las Vegas, Nevada: Stanley W. Paher, 1981.

Mitchell, John D. *Lost Mines & Buried Treasures Along the Old Frontier.* Glorieta, New Mexico: The Rio Grande Press, Inc., 1953.

Paine, Ralph D. *The Book of Buried Treasure.* New York, New York: The MacMillan Company, 1926.

Parris, Preston. *Treasures in the Sand.* Atlanta, Georgia: T.R.H. Hunter Publishing, 1991.

Penfield, Thomas. *Dig Here.* San Antonio, Texas: The Naylor Company, 1962, 1966.

Penfield, Thomas. *A Guide to Treasure in California.*
Deming, New Mexico: Carson Enterprises, 1982.

Pepper, Choral. *Treasure Legends of the West.* Layton, Utah:
Gibbs Smith, 1994.

Perrin, Rosemarie D. *Explorers Ltd. Guide to Lost Treasure in
the United States and Canada.* Harrisburg, Pennsylvania:
Stackpole Books, 1977.

Prassel, Frank Richard. *The Great American Outlaw.* Norman,
Oklahoma and London: University of Oklahoma Press,
1993.

Pringle, Patrick. *Jolly Roger.* New York, New York:
W. W. Norton and Company, Inc., 1953.

Randle, Kevin D. *Lost Gold & Buried Treasure.* New York,
New York: M. Evans and Company, Inc., 1995.

Rhodes, Bernie A. *D. B. Cooper, The Real McCoy.* Salt Lake
City, Utah: University of Utah Press, 1991.

Rieseberg, Lieut. *Harry E. Fell's Complete Guide To Buried
Treasure, Land and Sea.* New York, New York: Frederick
Fell, Inc., 1970.

Riley, Dan; Primrose, Tom; and Dempsey, Hugh. *The Lost
Lemon Mine.* Calgary, Alberta: Frontiers Unlimited,
1963.

Sabin, Edwin L. *Wild Men of the Wild West.* New York, New
York: Thomas Y. Crowell Company, 1929.

Schurmacher, Emile C. *Lost Treasures and How to Find Them.*
New York, New York: Paperback Library,

Smith, Alan. *Introduction to Treasure Hunting.* Harrisburg,
Pennsylvania: Stackpole Books, 1971.

Snow, Edward Rowe. *Pirates and Buccaneers of the Atlantic
Coast.* Boston, Massachusetts: The Yankee Publishing
Company, 1944.

Snow, Edward Rowe. *The Romance of Casco Bay.* New York,
New York: Dodd, Mead & Company, 1975.

Snow, Edward Rowe. *True Tales of Buried Treasure*. New York, New York: Dodd, Mead & Company, 1951.

Taft, Lewis A. *Profile of Old New England*. New York, New York: Dodd, Mead & Company, 1965.

Tatham, Robert L. *Missouri Treasures and Civil War Sites*. Raytown, Missouri: R. L. Tatham Co., 1982.

Terry, Thomas P. *World Treasure Atlas*. La Crosse, Wisconsin: Specialty Publishing Company, 1978.

Titler, Dale M. *Unnatural Resources*. Englewood Cliffs, New Jersey: Prentice Hall, Inc., 1973.

Ulyatt, Kenneth. *Outlaws*. Philadelphia, Pennsylvania and New York, New York: J. B. Lippincott Company, 1976.

Various authors. *Historic Western Trails Vol.2 Gold Edition*. Portland, Oregon: Northwind Publishers, 1995

von Mueller, Karl. *The Treasure Hunter's Manual*. Alamo, California: The Gold Bug, 1966.

Wellman, Paul I. *A Dynasty of Western Outlaws*. Garden City, New York: Doubleday & Company, Inc., 1961.

Wendt, Ron. *Gold, Ghost Towns & Grizzlies/Treasure Hunting in Alaska*. Wasilla, Alaska: Goldstream Publications, 1994.

Williams, Brad & Pepper, Choral. *Lost Treasures of the West*. New York, New York: Holt, Rinehart and Winston, 1975.

Wilson, Ian. *Undiscovered*. New York, New York: Beech Tree Books/William Morrow, 1987.

Magazine references:

Duffy, Howard M. "Big Treasure in a Little County." *Lost Treasure,* November 1996, 47-48.

Goldberger, Herb. "Louisiana's Famous Treasures." *Lost Treasure,* June 1998, 48-49.

Manwin, John K. "Coins of the Sevier Desert." *Lost Treasure,* August 1996, 16-18.

Pallante, Anthony J. "Colorado." *Lost Treasure*, October 1998, 22-25.

Pallante, Anthony J. "Delaware." *Lost Treasure*, June 1996, 25.

Pallante, Anthony J. "Illinois." *Lost Treasure*, July 1998, 36-39.

Pallante, Anthony J. "Indiana." *Lost Treasure*, May 1997, 18-22.

Pallante, Anthony J. "Iowa." *Lost Treasure*, June 1996, 36-39.

Pallante, Anthony J. "Maryland." *Lost Treasure*, May 1997, 40-43.

Pallante, Anthony J. "Michigan." *Lost Treasure*, March 1997, 28-33.

Pallante, Anthony J. "Minnesota" *Lost Treasure*, January 1998, 52-54.

Pallante, Anthony J. "Mississippi." *Lost Treasure*, February 1996, 28-33.

Pallante, Anthony J. "Kansas." *Lost Treasure*, February 1998, 52-54.

Pallante, Anthony J. "Nebraska." *Lost Treasure*, November 1998, 27-29.

Pallante, Anthony J. "New Jersey." *Lost Treasure*, April 1996, 44-47.

Pallante, Anthony J. "New Jersey." *Lost Treasure*, January 1999, 14-16.

Pallante, Anthony J. "North Dakota." *Lost Treasure*, July 1998, 23-25.

Pallante, Anthony J. "Ohio." *Lost Treasure*, September 1997, 40-43.

Pallante, Anthony J. "Utah." *Lost Treasure*, March 1996, 48-51.

Pallante, Anthony J. "Vermont." *Lost Treasure*, April 1999, 12-13.

Pallante, Anthony J. "Wisconsin." *Lost Treasure*, November 1997.

Rego, Anthony J. "The Mulliner Gang Cache." *Lost Treasure,* April 1999, 44-45.

Revis, B. G. "Gold to the Max." *Lost Treasure,* July 1997, 19.

Revis, B. G. "Treasures of the Great Lakes." *Lost Treasure,* July 1998, 27-29.

Wamsley, James S. "Brethren of the Coast." *Coastal Living,* September-October 1998, 46-54.

Today's Treasure Hunter. Oscoda, Michigan: Amateur Treasure Hunter's Association, Inc. 1971.

Television references

Writer/Producer: Caras, Mark. A&E. "Biography. Ma Barker, Crime Family Values." 1997.

Executive Producers: Haffner, Craig and Lusitana, Donna E. A&E. "Treasure! The Lost Dutchman Mine." 1998.

Executive Producers: Haffner, Craig and Lusitana, Donna E. A&E. "Treasure! The Money Pit on Oak Island." 1998.

How I Got the Idea for This Book

I first became interested in lost treasures when my husband, George, told me about the famous treasure at Oak Island. He had visited the Oak Island site in Nova Scotia, Canada, when he was twenty-two years old.

On a recent vacation, we decided to learn more about local treasures, so we searched for old gold mines and lost treasure sites in California and Nevada. First, we drove down California's Highway 49, which was named for the 1849 California gold rush. There are several small mines along this highway. Some of these are now parks or museums, which offer historic tours about mining. One park we enjoyed was the Empire

Mine State Historic Park in Grass Valley, California.

Next we visited Sutter's Mill, where gold that began the California gold rush was first discovered by James Marshall in 1848. The mill is located along the South Fork American River at Marshall Gold Discovery State Historic Park, south of Coloma, California. Many people still pan for and find gold in this area. In fact, the weekend we visited, an international gold-panning competition was being held at the park. We even found gold flakes and two tiny gold nuggets ourselves that day in the river, not far from the Sutter's Mill sign.

Finally, we visited Virginia City, Nevada, where the most valuable discovery of silver on record was made by Henry Comstock in 1859. This discovery is known as the Comstock Lode. Today, tourists are allowed to go in a few old mine shafts along with guides. It was interesting, but dark and creepy, inside these cramped mine shafts. Some of them leaked water and were propped up by old, rotting wood timbers. They were not places to venture inside alone or without a flashlight. When our guide told us ghosts had been spotted in the shafts over the years, the mines suddenly seemed even spookier!

By the time our vacation was over, I was hooked. I wanted to learn more about lost mines and treasures. At the library I found lots of information and was amazed to discover that there were so many lost treasure stories. There seemed to be at least one for every state in the United States. That gave me the idea for this book.